Introduction

This book is about creativity, what it is, what it is not and what you can do to become more creative. We'll also look at how to practice the guitar effectively (after all, what's the point in being creative if you can't put that into practice on your guitar?), how to learn effectively and a few practical points on guitar and guitar equipment.

Creativity and how to practice effectively is a widely misunderstood subject, people will write themselves off as not being creative before they have given themselves a chance, and give up on playing the guitar because they don't understand how to practice effectively and as such, do not make any progress.

I hope that by writing this book, you will be encouraged to try out some of the ideas and either become creative or enhance the creativity that you already have.

Overview of This Book

This book is split into a few sections. We've already talked about what creativity is. We are going to extensively cover guitar practice and how to practice efficiently.

The biggest stumbling block that most people have to being creative is that they don't know enough or have their skill level high enough. All knowledge and skills are in a hierarchy, as we ascend the hierarchy of ability/knowledge, we can tie together different concepts and ideas more effectively… which is another way of saying, we can become more creative.

After discussing how to practice effectively, we will look at what it is you need to do with that practice to be creative. We will also look at several "Creativity Tools" that I have developed over the years of teaching. We will cover how to learn effectively.

Hopefully, you will find that, after reading this book, you have a better idea of what creativity is and how you can go about being more creative.

Section 1: An Overview of Creativity

What Creativity Is Not

While I don't want to be too negative, it's important to clear up some misconceptions as quickly as possible, by having a quick conversation about what creativity is not.

Creativity doesn't "come out of nowhere". Creativity isn't genetic - people aren't born with a creativity gene or a guitar-playing gene. You aren't too old to be creative. There is no such thing as talent or natural ability, there is only practice (this has been proven[1,2]).

Anyone who chooses to read a book about creativity (or read in general) is intelligent enough to be creative.

What Is Creativity?

So what is creativity?

Oxford languages define it as:
"the use of imagination or original ideas to create something; inventiveness."[3]

According to Wikipedia, creativity is:

---

1 The Talent Code, Daniel Coyle

2 Bounce, Matthew Syed

3 Google search for define:creativity on 30th June 2022.

"**Creativity** is a phenomenon whereby something new and valuable is formed."[4]

and finally, the Cambridge Dictionary defines creativity as:

"the ability to produce or use original and unusual ideas"[5]

From looking at these definitions, we can see that creativity involves the creation of new ideas.

When we think about new ideas there are two types:

- Original Ideas
- Synthetic Ideas

Original ideas are truly new ideas. They are generations ahead of their time. When we think of creativity, people often tend to think about this. For example, inventing the lightbulb, or discovering calculus.

Synthetic ideas are ideas that combine previous ideas to create something new. For example, take something you already eat, such as roast beef, and put it in a sandwich to create a roast beef sandwich.

The majority of new ideas are synthetic ideas. You can think of this as standing on the shoulders of giants.

This gives us a clue as to what is involved in creativity. If we are going to combine ideas that others have created, we need to understand them. This is why learning and studying is a fundamental pillar of creativity, one that is often overlooked.

After all, when we think of creativity, we rarely think about someone sitting down and studying!

---

[4] https://en.wikipedia.org/wiki/Creativity accessed on 30th June 2022.

[5] https://dictionary.cambridge.org/dictionary/english/creativity accessed on 30th June 2022.

When it comes to discussing creativity, often we find the discussion ends here, if it gets this far at all.

But there is another step that we need to take.

Now we know that creativity involves working with ideas and creating new ideas, a question we should ask is “How do we go about creating new ideas?”.

New ideas are the same thing as problem-solving.

Fundamentally, creativity boils down to problem-solving.

Creativity comes about from asking a question and seeking the answer.

The question could be a simple one, such as, "What notes should I play over a C chord?", or it could be more complex, such as “Can I compose a sonata with a main theme in the key of Am with the time signature 7/8, that modulates to a secondary theme in the key of A♭m with the time signature 11/16?”.

When we have a question such as the one I asked above with the sonata, we give ourselves a framework from which we can get our creative juices flowing and start working on creating.

What we are going to do with this book is break down, in detail, how this process works and what we can do to become more creative.

We’ll look at the errors that people commonly make when approaching creativity and practical steps that you can take to become more creative.

The Creativity Path

We can think of developing our creative abilities as a path, which has three main steps:

1. Studying Concepts
2. Guided Problem Solving

3. Self Directed Problem Solving

Let's briefly talk about each step:

Step 1: Studying Concepts

Studying concepts is fundamental to becoming creative. You cannot create new ideas without understanding the ideas that already exist.

We also want to avoid re-inventing the wheel. By studying techniques, ideas and best practices that already exist, we can "get up to speed" with our contemporaries and start working on something new.

Before becoming a musician and composer, I studied astrophysics at university, eventually gaining a master's in physics with astrophysics.

Up until my graduation, I thought of learning as regurgitating facts.

I thought that the point of studying was to memorise various facts.

I'm not sure if this is more damming of myself or the education system (probably a bit of both), but that's what I thought it was.

However, this is not what learning is about.

Learning is about understanding concepts, the context that particular concepts apply to and the essentials that define different concepts.

We are going to cover learning in quite some detail, from the epistemology behind concepts to practical ways you can improve your learning and what you should be learning.

Step 2: Guided Problem Solving

The next step to being creative is guided problem-solving.

If you have a teacher that is any good, after teaching you something they will get you to work on it.

If they are teaching you how to find the notes in a major chord, they will then give you a set of notes and ask what major chords they build, or give you a major chord and ask what notes it is made of.

Having the theory from studying the concepts is one thing, it is another to apply that to problem-solving.

The vital component here is that the problem-solving is guided - it is appropriate and directly applicable to what you have just been studying.

This idea has been understood for centuries by authors who write textbooks and leave a list of questions at the end of each chapter - those questions are guided problem-solving.

You can even take this concept and apply it to boxing. When a coach is looking for the first match for a new fighter, they don't go and put their rookie fighter up against the world heavyweight champion - they find someone suitable at their level.

Step 3: Self-Directed Problem Solving

This is the final step and often the most missed out step.

Once you have gone through steps 1 and 2, you want to start setting your own problems to solve or find ways to apply your new knowledge to problems that are different to the ones that your instructor or book has set.

This is where creativity comes into play.

To return to the example of major chords, after your instructor has covered the theory behind how a major chord works, you could then see how many different ways you could play them on guitar.

How many ways can you play them holding down all the notes in the chord at one time?

How many ways can you play a major chord playing each note one after the other?

How many ways can you play a major chord by using tapping?

You can quickly see that we can take the concept of a major chord and explode it into an enormous set of possibilities and problems to solve.

As you become more advanced in your understanding, you will find that the possibilities open to you become greater, which is why we have such a diverse amount of music today.

The Spiral Theory of Knowledge

Something worth mentioning before we move on is the "Spiral theory" of knowledge.

I first heard this formalised in a book called "Understanding Objectivism"[6], which is an edited transcription of a series of lectures that were built around psycho-epistemology, which is the study of how we approach thinking.

Often when thinking about the pursuit of knowledge, we think about it linearly, as a line from A to Z.

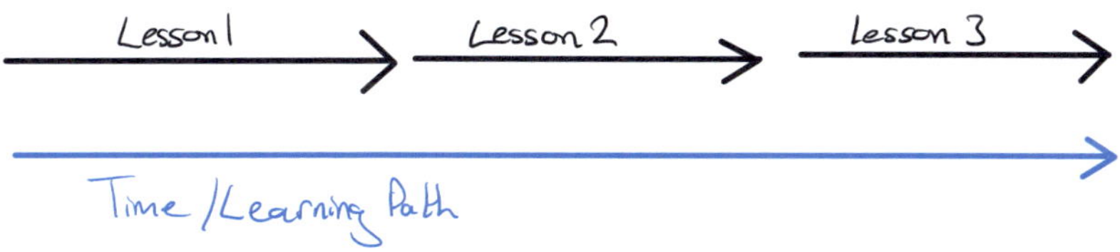

Linear Theory of Knowledge

---

6 Understanding Objectivism: A Guide to Learning Ayn Rand's Philosophy, 1st Edition, Leonard Peikoff (author), Michael S Berliner (Editor).

We start at A, then learn the different elements of our subject until we reach Z, at which point we “know” the subject. This is a “linear theory of knowledge”:

Instead, we want to think of the pursuit of knowledge like this:

We start at a dot, from which emanates several lines, which are the topics within our subject. We move in a spiral out from the centre, cutting through each line, progressively further along that line.

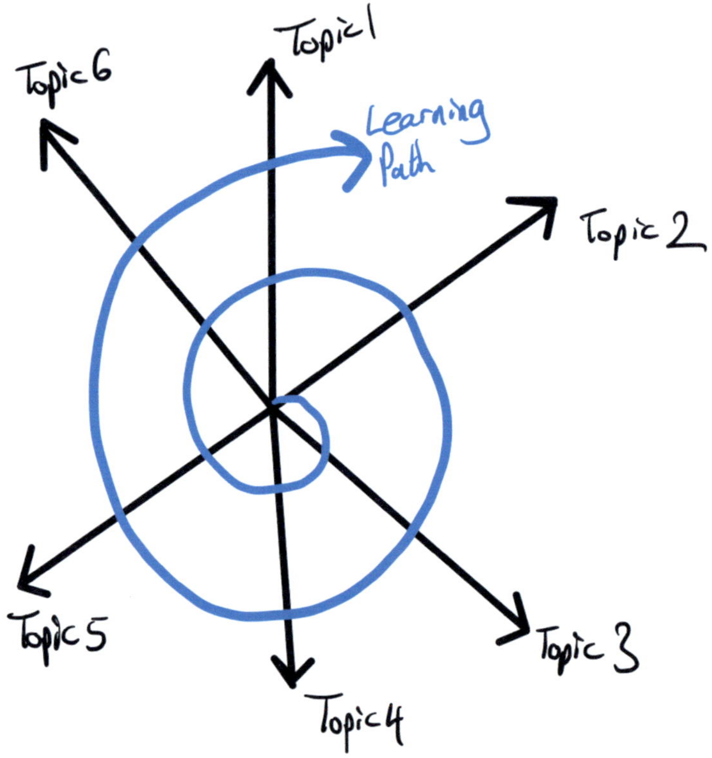

Spiral Theory of Knowledge

Each time we hit another line, we are repeating Steps 1 to 3.

In this manner, it is easy to understand that learning is a process and not an event. We don’t finish “learning music”, we don’t finish "learning guitar", and we simply move to the next point on our spiral, looking at more complex applications of ideas that we previously studied.

Other Factors That Impact Our Creative Potential

The creative path and the spiral theory of knowledge form the fundamentals of becoming creative, but many other factors can impact our creative potential, which includes our:

- environment
- approach to studying
- mindset
- health
- time management

and we are going to explore each of those, how they impact your creativity, and how you can use them to optimise your creativity.

Mindset Fundamentals

What is Mindset?

Mindset is how we think about something.

When it comes to creativity, we must approach it the right way.

Approaching creativity the wrong way leads to extreme frustration, which more often than not, leads to giving up entirely and regurgitating the mantra of "maybe I'm just not creative".

There are some basic approaches, or "best practices", that I have developed over the years, from reflecting on my behaviour and also from helping my students with problems that they face.

The Myth of Talent

The Difference Between Being Talented and Natural Talent

There are two ways of looking at talent – as a reflection of skill, or as a divine/genetic gift.

Talent as a Reflection of Skill

You might say that a "talented" person is someone who has achieved a very high level of skill. This could be a guitar player, a songwriter, an artist, an architect, or a salesperson; this could apply to any human skill.

The key idea here is that the talents in question have been achieved through deliberate practice by the individual in question.

Talent as a Divine / Genetic Lottery

The second way of looking at talent is the idea of "natural talent". This is the idea that talent comes from someplace that is external to you, that you have no control over. This could be divine, or genetic – two variables over which you have no control.

Natural talent is the idea that someone has an innate ability (i.e. genetic ability) with a skill. Natural talent is the idea that someone popped out of the womb with the ability to play guitar great from day 1. (Hopefully, you are already starting to see the idea doesn't make any sense…). This is a myth, there is no such thing as a gene that makes you great at playing the guitar.

Natural Talent Myths #1) Apples and Oranges Comparison

The first myth about talent we'll look at is a logical fallacy – the apples-and-oranges comparison.

We can go to a show, and watch someone like Steve Vai on stage play incredible music without missing a note. Everything he does looks flawless, it looks so easy; everything he does seems to flow… naturally.

But when we try to do it, when we learn, it's different. We struggle. It doesn't come naturally to us. Sometimes, we conclude that the person we are comparing ourselves to is naturally talented… and we are not.

The reasoning goes like this: It looks natural for Steve Vai to play, but it is not natural for me to learn, therefore Steve Vai must be naturally talented and I am not.

However, this is a logical fallacy. When we make this type of comparison, we are comparing two things that cannot be compared – our learning of guitar, to another person's performance *after* they spent time learning.

We are comparing the rate at which we learn, to the results of the time they spent learning.

These are two different things - it is illogical to compare them.

It doesn't make any sense to compare your ability at the start of learning something to the ability of someone who has been practising in that field for years.

Just like you wouldn't compare the price of a coca cola to the price of a gold watch, and say "This gold watch is expensive compared to a can of cola, therefore it is a bad deal", we can't compare how we learn to how someone else performs.

So what should we compare our playing against?

Compare your playing today, to your playing last week, and strive to improve it just a tiny bit. Just a little. If you strive to improve week by week and commit to learning for several years… you will not believe the levels of playing you can reach.

If you just keep going, improving week by week, you will be able to reach any level of playing that you could dream of.

Natural Talent Myths #2) Our Experience is Unique

"Oh but it's different for me".
Yeah? How do you know?
We are all individuals. We have our thoughts, values and ambitions. But we are also all human. We have a lot in common. We all need to eat a similar amount, drink a similar amount and maintain a certain core body temperature.

So the question is – is learning something that is a similar experience for most people? Do some people learn faster than others?

Or to get to the point, the question we often ask ourselves is:
"Why do I learn so slowly compared to everyone else?".

I'm going to say that, for most of the population, we learn at a pretty similar rate. However, some factors differ between people, which affect the rate of progress:

- How well we focus on a task
- The questions we ask ourselves while we are learning
- The amount of time we put into a task
- The mindset that we have in approaching a task
- Our environment when learning

Do you think Steve Vai picks 4 notes then neurotically worries that he did it wrong, and spends 3 hours googling the "right way to do it"? Or do you think he just gets on with it? While I can't say for sure, I'm guessing it's the latter.

Did Yngwie Malmsteen play the guitar for 10 minutes a day, or did he practice relentlessly, skipping school and falling asleep with his guitar?

These areas are all areas that we can actively improve, to learn guitar faster and reach higher levels of playing.

When it comes down to it, we all learn at pretty much the same rate. By improving the above areas, we accelerate our rate of progress.

"I get what you're saying, but what if I do learn slowly?"
There is one response, and two solutions to this problem.

The first is – you have to look at this like a mathematical equation. If you learn slowly, then you can still achieve high levels of playing by putting in more practice time which is high-quality practice.

Therefore, plan out ways to increase your practice time on guitar, and you can still achieve high levels of playing!

So what if you learn slowly? It doesn't matter.

The second way is to find a great teacher to help you. You might have to sift through a few different teachers to find one that works well for you. Having someone give you advice and feedback, answer your questions and help make sure that you correctly understand and practice various topics and have a plan for doing so; is a great way to accelerate your progress on the guitar.

But the truth of the matter is, you don't learn slowly. Every second you spend considering that thought is one you could have spent practising and improving. Ironically, worrying that you are a slow learner will slow down your learning!

Next time you catch yourself worrying about whether or not you are a slow learner, pinch yourself (literally) and just get back to practising the guitar.

Talent Myth #3) Expert Amnesia

Sometimes, talented people themselves spread the myth of talent. Have you ever watched instructional DVDs of great guitar players? I know I have… sometimes these DVDs really suck!
Let me clarify.

These DVDs have awesome licks and great ideas to work on, but they rarely explain how to play those awesome ideas. When some guitar players are asked how to play XYZ lick, they say "just do it". When they are asked how they learned, they say they just did it.

And boom – the myth of natural talent has new life.

However, this is not quite true. This is an effect referred to as "Expert Amnesia". This is when someone has reached an incredibly high level of ability and cannot remember what it is like to be at a lower level. This is why sometimes, high-level guitar players struggle to effectively teach beginner guitar players because it is incredibly difficult for them to understand things from the beginner's perspective.

You may have experienced this yourself when taking lessons. A teacher may give you something and tell you to play it, you struggle and then they get frustrated with you! I have one student, who had a previous teacher tell her that she probably wouldn't be able to play the guitar. She now writes her own music, can freely improvise across a variety of scales and is studying counterpoint. The problem wasn't her "natural ability" to play the guitar, it was that things were not sufficiently explained to her.

The effect of Expert Amnesia occurs partially due to the nature of how our minds work and how we learn. Additionally, this is not to say that all high-level guitar players are bad teachers!

Expert Amnesia, Epistemology and Tying Your Shoe Laces
Let's talk briefly about how we learn. We learn by taking simple ideas and integrating them into concepts. Then we learn more advanced ideas and skills, by integrating concepts.

For example, we learn to identify the colour brown, to identify the texture of wood and how to distinguish shapes together. When we see a certain arrangement of this sensory data, and we create the mental concept of a chair.

We learn what a chair is, what a table is, and what a bench is; and we integrate these low-level concepts, to form a slightly higher-level concept of furniture.

Learning guitar works the same way, but we have the added complexity of performing a physical action in addition to building mental concepts. There is a mechanical and a conceptual side to learning guitar, and they have to be worked on simultaneously.

As a guitar example, to pick through a 3-note-per-string scale, we have to train three separate skills:

- Picking notes on a single string
- Controlling how the pick travels between strings
- Visualising the scale position on the guitar neck

And then combine them, to effectively pick through a scale.
Now, imagine it took you several months to master the two basic motions of picking on a single string, controlling the movement of the pick between strings and visualising guitar scales in different keys.

Then you relentlessly shred scales for 20 years. It's easy to imagine that you might have forgotten what it was like to work on the fundamental building blocks of your technique.

Another possibility is that the guitar player in question did not consciously distinguish between each element of picking through a scale. They just did it a million times until something clicked, and they found they were able to shred their scales.

The advice someone in this situation would give, based on their experience, is that you "just" need to do it a million times. And while there is certainly a strong element of repetition needed to develop a skill, consciously identifying the components of that skill and working on them individually, then integrating them, will help you learn a lot, lot faster.

You Have Expert Amnesia Too
Take something you do every day, such as tying your shoelaces or brushing your teeth. Now write out a list of instructions on how to do that action.

Finally… follow your instructions exactly. Would someone who had never performed that task before be able to follow your instructions and accomplish the task?

If you wrote something like "Just do it"… then the answer is no! And you have expert amnesia. If you take 10-15 minutes, sat and thought, you could probably work out an effective list of instructions. You will probably find that your instructions need some testing to help you fully document the process of brushing your teeth.

Why Do We Get Expert Amnesia?
A fundamental part of what our brains do, and what learning is, is automating. We consciously train a skill and over time, and with enough repetitions, we eventually automate that skill, "forgetting" the fundamental components of the skill and retaining the higher-level outlook. As an example, we go from having to visualise the scale, move the pick between the strings and carefully fret the notes, to "just" playing a major scale.

This is a natural (and incredible) feature of how our minds work, which allows us to work on higher-level concepts and more advanced skills.

Ideas and Execution
This is quite a general idea we are going to look at.

Someone can explain an idea to you, and that idea may take 2 minutes to explain.

It could take 2 months… or 2 years to execute and put into practice.

For example, I can explain the fundamentals of sweep picking to you in about 15 minutes, covering all the vital aspects of the technique.

Properly learning that technique will usually take 6 - 9 months.

Why is that?

When we are learning a technique, we are forcing neural pathways in our brain to grow and re-enforce.

This is a physical process in our brain and it takes time to happen.

This may seem like a simple concept, but it's important because often people think that because they understand an idea, but can't execute the idea on the spot, they cannot execute the idea at all.

This is completely wrong!

Understand that your ability to understand an idea and perform the idea, while related, exist on completely different time scales. If you can grasp this, you will save yourself a lot of frustration.

Perfection as a Guide, One Step Farther as the Goal

This is a concept that we will revisit, possibly more than once, but I want to cover it here, as it is another big mindset idea.

Often when it comes to learning guitar, I see students try to get things perfect.

Now, I'm not saying don't try to get something perfect, but you have to understand that knowledge, and ability, are not linear (we previously looked at this with the spiral theory of knowledge).

Perfection is a curse that can affect you in your practice and your composition. Let's look at both.

Perfection in Your Practice

Often, a student will want to be able to play an exercise perfectly before moving on to the next exercise, or next lesson.

When you work this way, the 80/20 rule starts to work against you.

The 80/20 rule states that 80% of the results come from 20% of the work.

Or in reverse… the top 20% of results take 80% of the work.

In plain English, this means that getting an exercise to 80% takes 20% of the work, and getting that last 20% takes 80% of the work, i.e. the last little bit of exercise to reach "perfection" takes four times as much work.

In general, I find that getting an exercise to around 80%-90% and then moving on to the next helps students progress much faster than if they spend all their time on getting one exercise to 100%.

I also find that if a student is to practice this way for several weeks, they will find that when they revisit an older exercise they had at 80%, they can usually get it to 100% with relative ease.

As counter-intuitive as this sounds, it is very effective.

Perfection in Your Songwriting

Songwriting is a very personal experience, and releasing a song can be incredibly stressful.

You're taking something you've worked on and putting it out to the world.

This can be even worse in the modern-day setting of the internet and social media, with trolls and haters lurking in the void, waiting for the chance to tear down what you've put your work into.

I've experienced this myself. When before releasing my album Impetuous Desire, I listened to it every night before going to sleep for a month, wondering if it was good enough and if I should just delete it.

Fortunately, I "saw the light" and released it.

I know that students have felt anxiety about releasing music they have composed.

Maybe you can relate to how they feel.

Where does this anxiety come from? It can come from:

- comparing what we have composed and recorded to our favourite songs, then concluding that our song falls short.
- wondering "who we are" to go and release a song.
- identifying any minute errors in the song that no one else will ever hear or be able to hear.

So when it comes to composing and releasing your music, what should the standard be?

We do want to seek perfection but in our effort, not the product of our effort.

We can't guarantee that we will write a great song, but we can guarantee that we will put 100% into it, that we will apply ourselves in a focused way and throw everything we have at it.

That is the standard of perfection that we should adhere to.

Our job as composers is not to judge the output of our work, that is for the public to do.

Our job is to judge the standard of the effort we put into our work.

Additionally, consider this - if you try, you can probably write a song that is at least half decent.

Is there one person in the world who will enjoy listening to that song?

Is there one person in the world, who for a few minutes, you could make their life better by listening to your song?

Probably.

Given the population of the world and how tragically awful most modern music is, this is almost certainly true.

If you try and judge your music as good or bad, you will psychologically paralyse yourself. So don't do it!

The Speed You Can Work at Increases With Time

When you are at the start of your journey, the time it takes to complete projects can seem daunting.

Your first instrumental song may take you months to complete. You do some simple maths and extrapolate that it will take you 3 years to complete a short album.

That can be quite daunting.

At this point, it's easy to feel that the mountain ahead of you is insurmountable.

However, the above calculation fails to take into account how you will improve with time.

Sure, your first few songs will take you a few months to compose.

But after that experience, you'll be able to compose a bit faster - you'll learn workflow "hacks" that you can use to use your software faster. You'll learn more efficient ways to record. You'll learn more efficient ways to learn your compositions.

If you keep studying, you will learn faster ways of composing.

You'll become more solid with your understanding of the fundamentals that go into composing, speeding up the rate at which you can compose.

Your playing and performance skills will improve, meaning that you no longer need 1021 takes to get a good recording of that difficult lick.

If you just keep working at it consistently, you will slowly and consistently improve over time.

As we mentioned earlier, if you stick to the process for a few years, you will find your ability to compose and record increases consistently, allowing you to work faster at a higher quality than before.

The Myth, and Danger, of Going "All In"

You don't have to look far in the creative world to find the advice of "going all in". The gurus and experts pedal this, as well as their lackeys.

Why is this a myth, and why do people keep pushing this idea?

The Myth

Succeeding in any creative venture takes time, and a bit of luck.

You can be a great composer, but there might not be an audience for what you create, or if there is an audience, developing that audience may take time.

There is one inescapable truth - you're going to need money to live. You need a roof over your head and food on your table. Other people create these things and you need to make money so that you can trade for them.

If you go "all in", you find yourself with a lot of time, which is great for creating, but without an income, which is not so great for living.

A more effective approach is to keep a day job so that you can pay for your life, and work on your composing as a side project until it takes off (if that's what you want).

Why Does This Myth Keep Going?

This myth is often perpetuated by the "marketing gurus", as a way to guilt you into being "serious" about your music… and buying into their programs.

They'll roll out the story of the commander who ordered his troops to "burn their ships" to force them to win the battle.

Unfortunately, all that you get from this is losing a big chunk of change and putting yourself in a financially precarious position.

Section 2: Guitar Practice

In this section, we are going to take an in-depth look at guitar practice. We are going to break down how to approach and organise your practice, and what it is we are trying to achieve with practice.

Implementing all the ideas in this section will take time. The most effective way to use this section of the book is to read through it and pick one idea that you think will help you the most. Take a week to implement that idea into your practice. Then the following week, pick another idea and then incorporate that into your practice.

Muscle Memory

What is it we are trying to achieve when we practice the guitar? Most of the time, we are working on training what is known as "muscle memory", which is our ability to play something accurately, with little effort and without having to think about it.

There are four levels to mastering any physical skill:

- Conscious incompetence
- Conscious competence
- Subconscious incompetence
- Subconscious competence

Level 1: Conscious Incompetence

At level 1 we are carefully thinking through the movements we are trying to execute and our body is not doing what we what. We are trying to make the chord change and our fingers are flying everywhere. We are trying to pick through a scale and our pick hand is hitting all sorts of strings it shouldn't be. This is the level that we all start at when working on a skill.

It is vital to practice slowly, you must practice slowly enough that you give yourself enough time to think through what you are doing. You may find it helpful to talk yourself through what you are trying to do out loud, to force yourself to slow down to the speed at which you can think.

It is common for students at this level to try to practice too quickly. By playing too quickly, their mind can't consciously think through what they are trying to do, forcing their mind to rely on their subconscious skill, which has not yet been trained, and predictably, nonsense comes out of their hands.

Progression to level 2 requires slowing things down, way down, so you can think through what you are doing.

Play things slow enough to get them right. If you are consistently making mistakes, you are playing too quickly and not learning anything.

Level 2: Conscious Competence

At this level, we are still carefully thinking through what we are doing, but we are now executing movements accurately and the music is starting to sound "right". You will probably find that you can think things through a bit faster than when you were at level 1.

Here it is tempting to start speeding things up - but resist the urge to move too quickly! Now that you can consciously play the exercise accurately, start to think about muscle tension and technique - are you playing things as efficiently as you could be, or are you waving your hands around? Are you relaxed when you play or is your body tense like you're about to fight a bear?

Working on your technique and muscle tension will help you progress to the next level. It is also important to play the exercise at the same tempo, accurately, the same way, every single time. At this level, we are trying to "program" our muscle memory.

You can think of programming muscle memory like this: You have to play something 10 times in a row, correctly, exactly the same way to increase your muscle memory by 1. During those 10 repetitions, if you make a mistake or play something a different way (for example, but using a different finger), you "reset" your repetitions and have to start again.

A common mistake is to play an exercise slightly differently each time the exercise is repeated. This forces your muscle memory to have to learn three... four... five different ways of playing the exercise, which makes programming the muscle memory infinitely harder.

Level 3: Subconscious Incompetence

This level is usually a sign that we have rushed level 2. Now, there is a fine line that has to be drawn here, which I'll attempt to explain. At some point, we have to push the tempos of what we are working on and push ourselves to the next level. We also have to ensure that we can play something correctly before doing so.

When pushing ourselves appropriately, it can take a few repetitions to get the hang of what we are doing, after all, our body doing something "new" by increasing the tempo, so it is unreasonable to expect to play the exercise perfectly the first time we increase the tempo.

However, if we are unable to play at a higher tempo, we need to come back down a bit.

When increasing tempos, I usually find 15-20 repetitions will give me a good idea of if I need to turn the metronome back down or soldier on. If, after 15-20 repetitions, you see no improvement, you need to slow things back down. If you see a lot of improvement, you probably want to continue pushing to get it right. If you see a little improvement, maybe find a tempo between where you were and where you are.

Level 4: Subconscious Competence

At this level, we can truly say that the skill has been "learned", and we can move on to something else, creating a variation of it, pushing the tempos even harder, or trying it out in different contexts. At this level, we can see big improvements in the speeds we can reach, while still playing accurately.

I usually find this level takes 2-3 weeks to reach, practising an exercise 6 days out of 7.

Side Note on Pushing Tempos

It is worth pushing your ability beyond what you can do. If you find you are struggling at say, 100bpm, then having a go at 110bpm for 5-10 minutes, where you try and force your body to play faster, can be beneficial, when you roll the tempo back down to 100bpm you may well find that it is now a bit easier.

However, if you spend all your practice time at 110bpm, you will be wasting time.

If you play electric guitar, a great training trick is to warm up with the exercise on an acoustic guitar - acoustic guitar strings are much bigger and heavier than electric guitar strings, making the exercise much harder. Take your exercise and play it on acoustic guitar for 5 minutes. Then go back to electric guitar. Your fingers will feel like they are playing faster than ever.

Preparing For Practice

Often we don't think of what it takes to prepare for practising and want to dive straight into rushing through the practice as fast as possible.

This is a huge mistake, and while rushing in like this gives you a feeling of being "busy" and "Getting things done", what you'll find is that you frustrate yourself, learn inefficiently with the wrong expectation and make very little progress.

That's why this section of the book deals with some of the ideas behind why we practice, what we are trying to achieve when we practice and how to set ourselves up to learn effectively long term, continuously making progress with our playing.

The Important of Long Term Learning

When it comes to learning guitar, or anything else in life, we often overestimate how quickly we can learn.

Tony Robbins has a fantastic quote on this, "We overestimate what we can accomplish in a year and underestimate what we can accomplish in 10", and learning guitar is a great example of the power of this concept.

I cannot count how many times I have seen a student say something along the lines of, "This is simple I should be able to just play it". Simple by what standard? Just because you understand what your fingers should be able to do, does not mean that they will do it - every single motion you want to make on a guitar must be trained.

And to demonstrate the other side of the spectrum, I have students who when at their initial lesson thought that writing their own guitar song would be impossible, 7 years later, are composing their own orchestral works and performing their own arrangements of jazz standards.

Most people give up early and don't truly apply themselves to learning something long-term.

They might dip into it from time to time and play a few chords, but they don't truly stick to learning long-term.

The truth is, if they did, and if you stick to learning long term, you would not be able to imagine the progress you would make across 5… 10… 15 years…

This is important to understand: Anyone who sticks to something long-term and takes their learning seriously is going to make incredible progress.

Someone studying in academia will spend 7 years going from undergraduate to acquiring a PhD in their chosen field. Sticking to aggressively learning and practising for 7 years… 10 years… 15 years… is like acquiring your own PhD in guitar and composition.

Sure it's not exactly the same, but given some of the subjects people seem to gain a doctorate in, it's a better use of your time!

Why Do People Quit Learning Guitar?

So when it comes to dedicating ourselves to something long term, even if it's something we enjoy, or at least think we will enjoy, why do people quit before giving themselves a chance?

There are a few reasons:

- Not budgeting their time
- Not understanding what learning "feels" like
- The difference between practising and playing
- Not understanding how to learn
- Setting the wrong standard for evaluating their progress

Not Budgeting Their Time

Elsewhere in this book we're going to talk about how important budgeting our time is (by controlling our time we can control the person we become), but for now, we'll look at the basic idea: If you want to improve at something, you have to put time into practising it.

It doesn't matter if it's learning guitar, learning mathematics, becoming a better father, or becoming a carpenter; improvement requires practice which requires time.

If you have a schedule that has no available time for practice and you enrol in lessons, you are not going to improve.

In fact, you will probably create more stress for yourself, which you do not need!

If you want to improve, you first have to create the conditions for success, which in this case means finding a way to budget some time every day so that you can practice.

Sit down with your calendar and budget some time to practice, every day. And then stick to it.

Not Understanding What Learning “Feels” Like

Learning will often feel frustrating. Or is it?

When we are learning something new, we are trying to find a way to do something that we have never done before.

To understand this on a slightly deeper level, we need to understand what “doing something” means on a neurological level.

Whenever we make an action with our body, a series of neurones in our brain fire in a specific sequence, which creates the electrical signal that makes our muscles move in a certain way.

When we are experts at something, such as tying our shoelaces or putting on a jacket, our brain has an established network of neurones to fire for that specific task.

As a task is practised over and over, the network involved becomes reinforced and the electrical signal can travel faster through it.

If we have never done that particular task before, that network does not exist and needs to be made.

This is what we are doing when we practice, we are forcing our brain to physically build new connections between neurones.

We are trying to force electrical signals around our brains in ways that are new to us.

This is difficult. We feel a mental resistance that takes focus to overcome.

This resistance is often misidentified as frustration.

That resistance is normal and should be expected. We should embrace it, because when you feel that resistance, it means you are right at the edge of your ability, which is the right place to be when learning something new!

But… a lot of people interpret this feeling as something negative and put a negative value judgement on themselves from it.

This feeling you experience when working on something new, such as a new chord progression, isn't a sign that you are stupid, that you have no talent, or that you can't play the guitar; it's a sign that you are doing exactly what you need to be doing to improve!

Changing how you emotionally react to this "resistance" is key to being able to push your ability long-term.

Sure it can be frustrating, but if it gets too much, walk away for five minutes, make a cup of tea and get back on it.

Don't give up because you are experiencing what it feels like to learn.

Practice Doesn't (Always) Have to be Fun

When approaching something like learning an instrument, we learn it because we want to get an emotional reward of some sort.

For most people, that's having fun.

However, reaching the stage where we can have fun takes effort, and that process usually isn't fun, at least, there are times when it isn't fun.

I know that sometimes I just don't want to pick up my guitar at all. Admittedly, this is rare, but sometimes I really have to make myself do it.

When I'm feeling like that, I don't usually have fun playing the guitar, but I know I need to at least do something, so I do something. I also know that when I sit down and work on something, the next day I am much better at it.

Other times, I can easily pick up the guitar, but there are things I need to practice that aren't very fun for me to do so, but I know will benefit me if I do.

And a lot of times, I really enjoy practising.

The point is, practice isn't always fun. Most of the time it should be a sort of rewarding concentration, sometimes practice puts us in an almost trance-like state.

But it isn't always fun, and that's ok. It is important to anticipate that it won't always be fun so that when this happens to you, rather than getting carried away in the emotion, you understand it and do some practice anyway.

The Difference Between Practising and Playing

This is a progress killer - a lot of the time when people pick up their guitars thinking they're practising, they're actually playing.

Playing guitar is when you are repeating a set of motions that you have previously learned.

Practising is when you are training your body on a new set of motions (these could be variations on something previously learned or something new).

If you look at how much time you are "practising", you will probably find you are playing and not doing much practice at all.

If you are not practising, you are not improving!

Now, I'm not saying that you should spend all your time practising and don't spend any time playing your favourite songs, but if you want to continuously improve your playing, you need to ensure that there is a proportion of your time devoted to practising, and generally speaking, the more time practising the faster you will improve.

Not Understanding How to Learn

This is a critical piece of the puzzle that we will cover in detail later in the book.

If you do not understand how to learn, or what the purpose of learning is, then you will not progress and you will not have fun.

It's as simple as that.

Unfortunately, we are never taught how to learn effectively. In school, we are taught that the process of learning is the memorisation of almost random facts.

This is simply not true.

Memorisation is a part of learning, but learning also requires integration and application, it requires understanding the context of the facts that you are studying and identifying the essentials behind each idea; and without these critical parts, your learning will be ineffective.

Setting the Wrong Standard for Progress

This one is killer.

When we set the wrong standard for "being able to feel good" about our playing, we are setting ourselves up to feel miserable about our playing… for life.

It doesn't take too much imagination to picture that someone who feels miserable about playing an instrument will not want to play it for very long.

When it comes to learning an instrument, 99% of students will compare themselves to their favourite player. They are continuously judging their ability against someone who is a master of their craft.

Unsurprisingly, they continuously come up short.

Let's make a comparison. Let's say it's your first day at university and your lecturer was giving you a brief overview of a complex topic that you will be studying later in the year.

It's obvious your lecturer is an expert in this field.

Would you feel like a failure because you don't know what your professor does?

Of course not! That would be ridiculous.

As soon as you think about this for one second, it's obvious that to feel bad because you don't know as much as the expert makes no sense whatsoever because you haven't put in the time like they have… which is why you're there in the first place!

Yet, when it comes to learning guitar, we do this all the time.

And because we do this, we make ourselves feel miserable.

So the question is, how should we judge our progress?

Should we judge our progress at all?

We need to find some metric to evaluate our progress, otherwise, we risk never improving.

The correct metric that we should use is how we were doing last week.

And the correct goal is to be a tiny bit better than we were last week, maybe just 1%.

That could be 1% faster with our tempo or playing 1% more consistently, or 1% less tension… you get the idea.

We just want to be 1% better.

Along as you are practising regularly, this is an achievable goal, in fact, most weeks you will improve more than 1%.

So, if you can retrain the criteria for what it takes to "feel good" about your playing from "Can I play like my favourite player?", to "Did I improve 1% compared to last week?", then you are going to feel good about your playing.

The impact of this is that if you feel good about your playing, you will keep practising and keep improving a few percent each week… over a period of several years.

And all those small improvements will compound into improvements so large that it's difficult for you to imagine at this point in time - if you just keep going, improving a little week by week, you will become a monster guitar player.

Setting the Correct Expectations of Ourselves

One question students often ask is, "How long does it take to learn guitar?". That's a bit like asking "How long is a piece of string?". It depends on many factors, all of which we will cover throughout the course of this book.

In general, if you are serious about your guitar playing, learning the guitar is a lifelong endeavour. It will take a lifetime to study and learn the various aspects of playing the guitar.

You can't control how fast you learn, but you can control:

- The amount of time you put into practice
- Your focus during practice
- What you practice

And, generally speaking, when you maximise those things, you learn faster.

If you set yourself a goal of "I want to learn 20 chords in the next five weeks", you may be disappointed when you don't reach that goal, you can't control how quickly you learn how to play chords (saying that, we will look at a few exercises later in the book that always work for speeding up how quickly you can learn chords).

If you set yourself the goal of "I will spend 45 minutes a day, at 8am, working on my chords", that is a goal that you can achieve. And by doing that, you should be able to improve a little bit on where you were last week, hitting that 1% weekly improvement goal we talked about in the previous section.

When it comes to general practice and technique, that is the method I would use for deciding how successful my practice has been - my goal is the time spent practising and the quality of the practice, not reaching a particular milestone. However, if I am failing to improve, then that tells me I need to change what I'm practising.

Every now and then certain events will happen where you have to perform - you'll have a gig, recording deadline, studio time booked; something like that. In those situations, you want to ramp up your practice so that the weeks before the event you are practising like mad. The night before and the day of the event do light warm-ups but focus on relaxing rather than intensity - save the intensity for when it's time to perform.

To revisit the original question of "How long does it take to learn guitar?", while we can't say how long it takes to learn guitar, we can look at how long some pieces take to learn.

Sometime around 2016, I was working on learning Bach's 1st and 2nd Cello Suite's. I booked a weekend of lessons with the artist known as "The Commander in Chief" - she's an electric guitarist who plays virtuoso violin pieces on guitar. While talking in general about music, I was staggered to learn that classical violinists will spend a year studying a single piece of music (that won't be the only thing they will learn, but they will spend a year working on it).

Before that, I had never considered that I should spend so long learning a piece of music… or that it was normal to spend so long learning a piece of music.

That's probably why these violinists are so good - if you work at anything for a year, you will find that you start to get pretty good at it!

This is a long way of saying, when it comes to working on something, don't feel down if it takes you a long time to learn it. It's not taking you a long time, it's taking you a normal amount of time to learn.

Why do we Judge Ourselves so Harshly?

Have you ever found yourself thinking, “This is simple, why is it taking me so long to learn it?”. I bet you have, every guitarist has thought that (I still battle fighting this thought).

I find many students suffer from this idea and it’s quite insidious - it leads to us feeling incompetent as guitar players, and feeling incompetent is not a good way to feel inspired to focus and practice.

So where does this idea come from and how can we fight it?

I think there are two possible causes:

- Conflating understanding an idea and performing an idea
- Not understanding what learning feels like

When looking at two chords on a page, we can usually conceptually understand what we have to do quite quickly, usually within a few seconds. We can read the tab or chord diagram and understand where to place our fingers and how to strum in order to play the two chords.

But making our body do that smoothly and in time is another matter. It takes time to train muscle memory and iron out any weird “bugs” in how we are moving between the two chords.

If we assume that the speed at which we can understand how to move our fingers should be the same as the amount of time it will take to train the movement of our two fingers, we will continuously be disappointed with ourselves.

Additionally, where does this assumption come from? Why should learning to move our fingers take the same amount of time as being able to read a tab? I have no idea about the source of this assumption, but by identifying it, hopefully, you can gain some serenity with your practice.

Another problem that adult students tend to face is that they have forgotten what learning feels like. We've already talked about this so we won’t cover it again. But to briefly mention, if you are not used to learning, you can make mistake the feeling of learning for the feeling of frustration/failure.

We constantly judge ourselves for not being able to play like XYZ guitarist. Sure, we might not be able to play a song as our favourite player does now… but that doesn't mean that we can never play the song like them, we just need to practice a bit more.

As a final thought on this topic, anytime we learn something new, even if it is composed of things we already know, we have to mentally treat it like learning from scratch. If you know the chords Em, G and D; it may be tempting to think that you "should" be able to play them in any order, at any time. Let's say you've been playing those chords for years but never played them in the following order: G - D - Em. You try that, struggle to get it as good as you want and feel miserable because you think you should be able to do it.

If you instead treated it as something new, you wouldn't be feeling miserable, and you'll practice it and eventually crack it.

Additionally, by what standard should you be able to learn it "quickly"? If you think about it, there are no facts supporting why you should "just be able to" do XYZ quickly. Have you scientifically measured how fast you can learn something new on guitar? Does learning one thing mean learning another should be any easier?

The thought of "this should be easy" is a complete fantasy with no basis in reality. It is ridiculous. Next time you feel that way, realise how ridiculous the idea is and throw it in the trash where it belongs, and instead, focus on your practice.

Organising Your Practice

There are five levels at which your practice can be organised, and to get the most out of your practice time, you need to consider all five levels:

1. What is the big-picture goal for whom you want to be as a guitar player?
2. How can you structure what you need to learn to achieve that goal (deciding on a learning path)?

3. How are you going to plan out your practice time every week?
4. What are you going to work on for the specific practice session you are about to have?
5. Feedback and improvement.

But before we do that, it is important to understand the difference between linear and non-linear practice - this is a direct reflection of the linear and spiral theories of knowledge that we looked at towards the start of the book.

Linear Practice

This is something that people into lead/shred guitar often fall victim to, and I know that I certainly fell prey to this trap.

Linear practice is when you practice one thing before moving on to the next. For example, you may want to practice rhythm guitar before learning lead guitar.

In my case, I always wanted to play as fast as possible, so I put years and years into developing my speed with scale sequences and sweep picking, completely neglecting my ornamentation (bends, slides and vibrato; how we play a note) skills.

I ended up being able to play over 16 notes a second… but my lead playing in general sucked, because I had no ornamentation skills. Fortunately, I since fixed that!

Linear practice often leads to a guitarist being very skilled in a very limited number of areas.

Unfortunately, as playing the guitar in "real" situations, for example, playing a song from start to finish or playing a nice guitar solo, involves combining a range of skills; the limited range of highly developed skills the guitar player can do are effectively worthless.

Non-linear Practice

This is a fancy way of saying practice several things at once. There is a balance to be struck, if you practice too many different things, then you end up in the reverse problem of the guitar player who practices linearly, where you practice so many different things that you are not skilled at any of them.

I usually find that when guitar players are wanting to work on their technique, having 3-7 different items to work on is the right balance.

If there is something in particular that you do want to be highly skilled at, for example, speed, then you could split your practice time between focussing on your speed and the rest of your time on a range of skills.

Setting Your Big Picture Goal

It's important to take a moment to think about exactly who you want to be as a guitarist. Someone who wants to learn to write and play funk music is going to have a different learning path than someone who wants to compose neoclassical guitar instrumentals for an orchestra.

Someone that wants to learn to play rock songs is going to have a different learning path than someone who wants to play jazz music.

Now, when starting, it can be difficult to visualise where you want to go with your guitar playing - part of the problem is that there are a lot of areas of guitar playing that you might not know about - there might be genres you haven't heard of, techniques you don't know about and you might have some misunderstandings about what's involved in certain aspects of playing.

But there will be something that takes your interest. You'll have music that you enjoy listening to, and maybe guitar players that you admire; so you can start there. Take something that holds your interest and move in that direction.

You can always change direction as you learn more about guitar and music, but to get started pick something - even if it's to learn three of your favourite songs.

When setting your goal, it should be something positive and concrete. For example, "I don't want to be a bad guitarist" is not positive or concrete. "I want to be a good guitarist" is positive, but it is not concrete, being "good" doesn't mean anything. "I want to be able to play 5 Iron Maiden songs" is positive and concrete. This is a goal that we can break down into steps and work towards.

Deciding on Your Learning Path

Now that you know where you want to go with your playing, you have to decide how to get there.

This has a bit of a catch 22 attached to it - you don't know how to get somewhere you have never been.

So you'll have to find someone who can offer you advice. You can use forums and Facebook groups. You might have some friends who play at a level that you want to play at whom you can ask for advice.

The most effective thing is to find a great teacher who can put together a plan for you. You don't necessarily have to take lessons with a teacher (although I would recommend that), but you could contact 2-3 teachers, tell them your big-picture goal, and then pay them to put together a plan for you.

Planning Your Weekly Practice Time

This is a big secret to effective practice: Plan your practice time. Create a schedule for your practice in advance that you will stick to.

I would go as far as writing down your schedule in your calendar, on paper or however you organise your life.

If you say to yourself, "I'm going to practice this week", and leave it at that, chances are you are not going to practice very much.

When planning your practice time, you want to aim to have frequent practice sessions, ideally every day, even if it is just for a few minutes. Practising for 15 minutes every day (105 minutes a week) will be more effective than practising for 3 hours once a week, even though practising for 3 hours once a week is more time in total than 15 minutes once a day.

This is due to several neurophysiological effects of how practice affects our brain that we will look at later in the book.

When planning your practice time, you always want to consider the time of day and what else is happening in your life.

For example, if you practice after work, you are going to be tired, hungry, distracted and a little stressed. If you practice before work, you are going to have your brain at maximum focus and you will be able to concentrate on what you are going.

So knowing that one of the most effective things you can do to improve your practice is to change your daily routine, go to bed a bit earlier in the evening and wake up earlier so that you can practice before work.

I know that is not possible for everyone, but if it is possible for you, then seriously consider it.

If you are wanting to make serious progress with your playing, you want to aim for a minimum of two hours of practice a day, 6 days a week. Make sure that if you do aim for this or more, you slowly build up to this much practice over several weeks, do not go from playing 0 minutes a day to playing 2 hours a day overnight.

How to Wake Up

Some people have a hard time waking up in the morning. I understand, it used to take me almost an hour to properly get my brain in gear in the mornings. I found the following things to help get my brain going as fast as possible:

- When you wake up, don't look at your phone. A lot of people will waste 20…30…60 minutes in the morning mindlessly on their phones. Leave it in a different room overnight, or at least away from the bed so you have to physically get out of bed before you can get to your phone.
- Get outside and take a 10-minute walk. No matter what the weather is. The sunlight, fresh air and light exercise will wake you up.
- Drink water - don't drink caffeine/coffee for 60-90 minutes after waking up. Or at least have a pint of water before your coffee.
- Consider quitting caffeine altogether, or at least switching to decaf. You'll probably sleep better after getting past the two-week detox hump.
- Do intermittent fasting (this is great because then you don't need to eat breakfast at all - massive time saver), or at the very least cut out the sugary cereals and carbs at breakfast and eat real food.

What Are You Working on For Each Specific Practice Session?

Now that you have planned your long-term goals, a way to reach them and when you will be practising, the last step is to think about what you will be practising in those scheduled practice sessions.

In general, I recommend having 3-7 "things" that you are working on with your playing at any one time. You want to ensure that your practice time is balanced appropriately, which is an ongoing skill.

Be careful with taking on more than 7 things to practice, you will end up not being able to spend enough time on any one item to improve at it.

I want to take a minute here to point out that there is no such thing as "the perfect practice routine", only "an appropriate practice routine for this point in time"; you will find that your practice routine changes and evolves as your abilities, goals and demands on your life change.

There are three ways you can consider organising your practice time:

- The Rotating Practice System
- A/B System
- One Item System

The Rotating Practice System

This system works best for people that are working on 3-7 different practice items, which are exercises to work on different skill sets and the person in question also has a fluctuating amount of time that they can practice for each day. We want to make sure that you can evenly practice all items.

Let's say there are 7 things you want to practice, practice items A, B, C, D, E, F and G. Let's also say that your weekly practice schedule looks like this:

Monday: 60 minutes

Tuesday: 15 minutes

Wednesday: 45 minutes

Thursday: 15 minutes

Friday: 30 minutes

Saturday: 60 minutes

Sunday: 45 minutes

I would practice your items for 15 minutes each as follows:

Monday: 60 minutes total: A, B, C, D

Tuesday: 15 minutes total: E

Wednesday: 45 minutes total: F, G, A

Thursday: 15 minutes total: B

Friday: 30 minutes total: C, D

Saturday: 60 minutes total: E, F, G, A

Sunday: 45 minutes total: B, C, D

This way, you rotate through your practice items evenly, ensuring that they all receive (nearly) the same attention.

You can physically organise this system by printing out, or writing down, your exercises. Have one page per exercise. Label each page if you want to and put them all on your music stand for practice.

Set your practice timer for 15 minutes and practice the exercise in front of you. When your timer goes off, move that exercise to the back of the pile, set your timer for 15 minutes and start on the next exercise. This system is incredibly simple and easy to follow. It allows you to sit down and get started with no preparation or fluffing around.

This system does not have to be rigid. When I was following this system several years ago, if I found myself having a breakthrough moment with a certain exercise and I was smashing my personal bests with the metronome, I would run with it for the rest of that practice session and see just how far I could go, then resume the rotation system the following day.

A/B System

This is effective for people that want to work on several areas of their playing and have a consistent practice schedule, where they can practice for roughly the same amount of time each day.

You break up your practice items into “Day A” items and “Day B” items, and your alternate between the two.

For example, you could have technique exercises on Day A, and a song you are learning to focus on for Day B.

This practice schedule allows you to work a little deeper on certain items than the rotating system.

One Item System

If you are practising for a gig or a recording session, then you will want to distribute your time differently, focusing on the project that you have to complete. Maybe you’ll be putting 75% of your practice time into practising songs and only 25% into working on your technique.

For this system, nearly all your time goes into practising for the project. I would still put some time, even if it is not much, into working on technique and other skills, even if it is just a warm-up exercise or two.

Which System is Right For You?

We’ve outlined three different systems for organising your practice. You’ll have to decide which one is best for you. Pick one system and stick to it for 2-3 months, then change it as you see necessary. You don’t have to stick to one system for the rest of your life, but you do want to stick to it for at least 2-3 months. You can create hybrids of these systems.

As with anything, think about what it is you are trying to achieve, figure out a way to do that, try a system out for a couple of months, and then assess how it’s going.

Feedback and Improvement

Whatever you are practising, you want to be aware of what it is you are doing. As obvious as that sounds, it can be surprisingly difficult - when you are focusing on trying to move your fingers in a certain way with something a bit new, it can be difficult to really listen to what you are doing and observe those motions objectively.

There will be things that you are aware of, and also things that you are not aware of. One benefit to having a teacher is you get instant feedback on what you are doing.

Another highly effective method of getting feedback is to record yourself. This will allow you to focus on listening so you can dissect what you are doing and figure out which bits of an exercise need the most work.

You will also find it beneficial to keep a short log of your practice. Record things like the maximum tempos that you reach and mistakes you are making. Is there a particular point of an exercise that you are consistently struggling with? A chord change that is a bit ropey?

Whatever feedback you are getting, whether it's from a teacher or your own video/audio recording, make notes on it in your practice log.

If you have printed your exercises on paper, you can keep a practice log on the back of each sheet. This way, when you next come to that practice item, you will know what it is you need to focus on. This also stops you from fiddling around with computer programs and keeps you focussed on the task at hand.

We will look at specific practice techniques later in the book.

How Much Should You Practice?

Practising more is better than practising less. If you want to play at the highest levels, then you'll need to be practising for a few hours a day, at least three. Steve Vai was famous for his immense 9 hour guitar workout that he used to do. Michael Angelo Batio would practice his picking for two hours every day to develop the insane speed he achieved. Yngwie Malmsteen would fall asleep with his guitar in his hands.

If you want to be at the top levels of playing, that's what it takes.

If you are a beginner, you want to build up your practice time over a period of weeks to months - going from practising for 10 minutes a day to practising for 10 hours a day will result in injuries.

Practising for extended periods is very taxing on the nerves, tendons and ligaments; and by increasing practice time over a longer period, you give the body a chance to strengthen these connective tissues.

If you are wanting to increase your practice time, do so in 15 minute increments, a week at a time.

If you want to increase your practice time faster, add extra practice time at opposite ends of the day. For example, if you practice for an hour in the morning, you could add a 30 minute practice session in the evening. By practising at opposite ends of the day, you give the body a chance to rest between sessions.

You also want to take micro-breaks when practising. For every repetition of an exercise, take 5 seconds to consciously relax your arms and hands. Every 10-15 minutes take a break, get up and walk for 10 seconds before getting started on the next practice item.

Once a week, I like to take a day off from practising to let my body rest. I'll also take days off as needed. For example, yesterday I was practising and started feeling a bit sore so I took the rest of the day off from practising.

Warning Signs of Injury

This and the following sections are not medical advice, just my experience.

It is possible to injure yourself from playing the guitar. This can be caused by practising too much and having bad technique can make this worse (see the appendix for the correct way to sit with your guitar).

Common injuries that guitar players get are tennis elbow and carpal tunnel syndrome. These are both quite serious problems that can be permanent.

More often than not, our body "warns us" before becoming injured, and it is important to be able to spot these warning signs.

If your fingertips are sore, that is ok. While I don't recommend it, you can lose skin and get blisters on your fingertips and while uncomfortable, this will heal.

If you ever feel shooting pains, stabbing pains (like someone has stabbed you with a pointy pencil), burning sensations or pins and needles; then you need to stop playing immediately and not play for the rest of the day. Usually, resting for the day (and maybe the next day) will leave you feeling fine.

Bathing the problem area in icy cold water for a few minutes after practice can help recovery.

Avoiding Injury

Doing a light yoga routine before and after practice can help prevent injuries. There are books and DVDs available on Amazon that cover yoga for musicians, any of them are probably fine. I've used a DVD called "Yoga for Musicians" by Penelope Roskell which I found very effective at a time when I was recovering from an injury.

When practising, take lots of little breaks. In the section on how to use a metronome properly, I advise that you have a bar of "count in" between repetitions of exercises - in addition to refocussing your mind and figuring out where the count is, you can use this as an opportunity to purposely relax your arms and hands before the next repetition starts.

Every 15 minutes, put the guitar down for a few minutes and have a stretch, walk to the kitchen and back or something, to get your body moving a little.

Again, when you start feeling warning signs of injury, put the guitar down. NEVER play through the pain - that is a stupid thing to do. I know, because I have made that mistake several times in the past, including one injury which meant taking several months off from playing the guitar so that I could recover, during which my arm was almost unusable.

If you do any tasks in your daily life that have a risk of RSI, such as a lot of typing, then research proper posture and technique to avoid repetitive injury. Make sure you take breaks. This will take some strain off your connective tissues and they won't be quite as "tired" when it comes to practising the guitar.

Recovering From Injury

If you do find yourself injured, seek help from a professional. I find that locating a good physiotherapist that specialises in musicians is the most effective treatment (depending on the injury - the injuries I have had to deal with have all been things that a physiotherapist specialises in).

Going private if possible is almost always better than waiting for government-provided healthcare, as you can be seen, diagnosed and start treatment almost immediately; rather than waiting for months on end. Going private can be expensive, but if possible, it is worth the cost.

You may want to seek two or three professional opinions before deciding on a course of action.

When I had my first serious guitar injury, I saw three professionals. The first recommended cortisol injections in my elbow. The next wanted to do a risky surgery to cut a piece of bone from my elbow. The next recommended a course of stretching, physiotherapy and yoga (mixed with some ultrasound treatment).

I started with the lowest risk recommendation (stretching, physio and yoga) which fixed me up nicely, within a few weeks. A professional is always going to speak from experience - surgeons know how surgery works, so if you see a surgeon they'll recommend surgery.

For some reason, the medical profession doesn't seem to be too aware of what physiotherapy can offer in terms of healing a patient. Whenever I get an injury, my physiotherapist is the first port of call.

How to Make Your Practice Time As Effective As Possible

So far we have discussed a lot of ideas around practice, but now we are going to dig into some of the tools, techniques and approaches you can use while practising that will make your practice time as effective as possible.

Use a Metronome

If you are not playing with a metronome, you are not playing in time, and playing in time is important!

We need to use a metronome because something every musician struggles with, guitar players included, is perceiving time accurately.

As an example, go back to the start of this article and try and count to 10 while reading it.

Or stop reading after 10 seconds.

Pretty tricky right?

We face a similar problem when playing the guitar, especially if we are working on new material - keeping track of time while our mind is focused on something we are learning is incredibly difficult.

I'm sure you've experienced working on some new chords, and you slip out of time without realising it when the chord changes come around.

The metronome gives us an external reference to make sure that our timing is accurate.

What is the Purpose of Using a Metronome?

Often, guitarists think that the purpose of using a metronome to practice is to play faster.

This is sort of true, but not quite.

The goal of using a metronome when practising the guitar is to play more accurately.

And once you can play accurately, you will find your speed naturally increases - think of speed as a by-product of accurate playing.

Speed is a by-product of accuracy. If you want to play guitar faster, learn to play more accurately.

There are several things involved with reaching high speeds with your lead guitar playing, and accurate timing is one of the most important.

Side note: You can check how fast you can play the guitar with our guitar speed calculator (https://www.study-guitar.com/guitar-speed-calculator/).

There is a second element to using a metronome.

In addition to wanting to practice playing accurately, we want to become comfortable at that tempo.

When learning to play a piece or exercise, we want to be able to play feeling relaxed, not tensed up, and not pushing the very limit of our ability.

Once we have achieved a level of comfort and reliability (ie being able to play the same exercise two-three times in a row without making mistakes), we can then increase the tempo.

So to summarise, our two goals with using a metronome are:

1. To play more accurately.
2. To become comfortable at a certain tempo.

The Top 10 Mistakes Guitarists Make When Using a Metronome

Here are some common mistakes that guitar players make when using a metronome, along with solutions that you can use today to help make your guitar practice more effective:

Mistake 1) Not Listening to the Metronome

This might be an obvious one, but you would be surprised how often it happens.

It is mainly a problem for beginner guitar players who aren't used to practising with a metronome.

When you use a metronome, you have to do two things at once – listen and play the guitar.

And doing these two things at once can be difficult.

It's common for a beginner to turn their metronome on, start practising… and the second they are playing the guitar, they stop listening to the metronome, quickly going out of time; or they'll play with the metronome for a few clicks and then "phase it out" in their mind.

Now, listening to a metronome and playing the guitar at the same time can be quite challenging, but make the mental push to listen to that metronome while you're playing!

Solution: Push your mental focus to the limit. Mental focus is like a muscle, it will improve with timing. The more you try, the easier it will become. SLOW THINGS DOWN, so it is easier to focus on all the things you need to do at the same time.

Jim Rohn has a great quote on this:
"Don't wish it were easier. Wish you were better."
But don't wish – practice.

Mistake 2) Not Leaving Breaks Between Repetitions

This sort of ties into the previous problem.

Sometimes when working on an exercise, a guitarist will use the metronome, they will be listening to it, and they will be playing repetitions of the exercise back to back.

The problem with this is that after a few repetitions it is quite easy to lose mental focus on listening and playing, and you slip into just playing without listening to the metronome.

Let's illustrate this idea with some tab. Let's say we were playing the following exercise:

A simple exercise to work through the first position of the A minor pentatonic scale, from the root note on the 4th string.

Now, when practising repetitions of this exercise, some guitar players may approach it as follows:

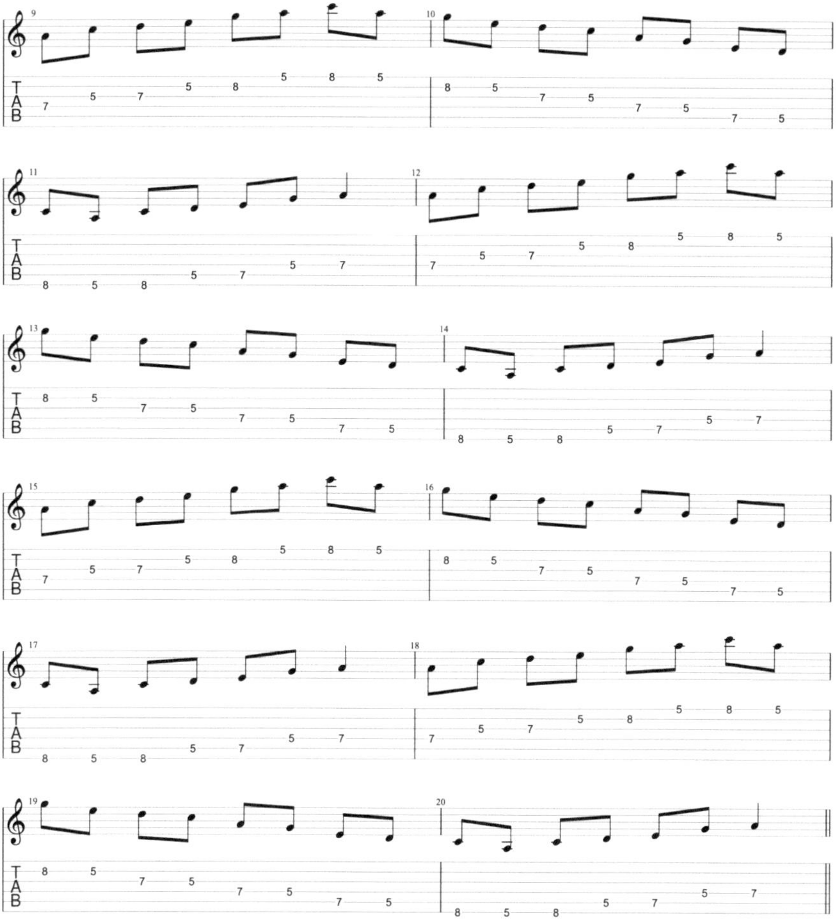

This is the same exercise as above, being played three times in a row. I recommend you do NOT take this approach when practising scales!

If you look through the tab and compare it to the three bar example that preceded it, you can see that we have taken the scale example and are playing it three times in a row.

I recommend you do not do this. It is easy to lose focus and slip out of time with the metronome.

Often when beginners slip out of time, they cannot get back in time... and then continue to play, out of time to the metronome.

A better way to approach this exercise is as follows:

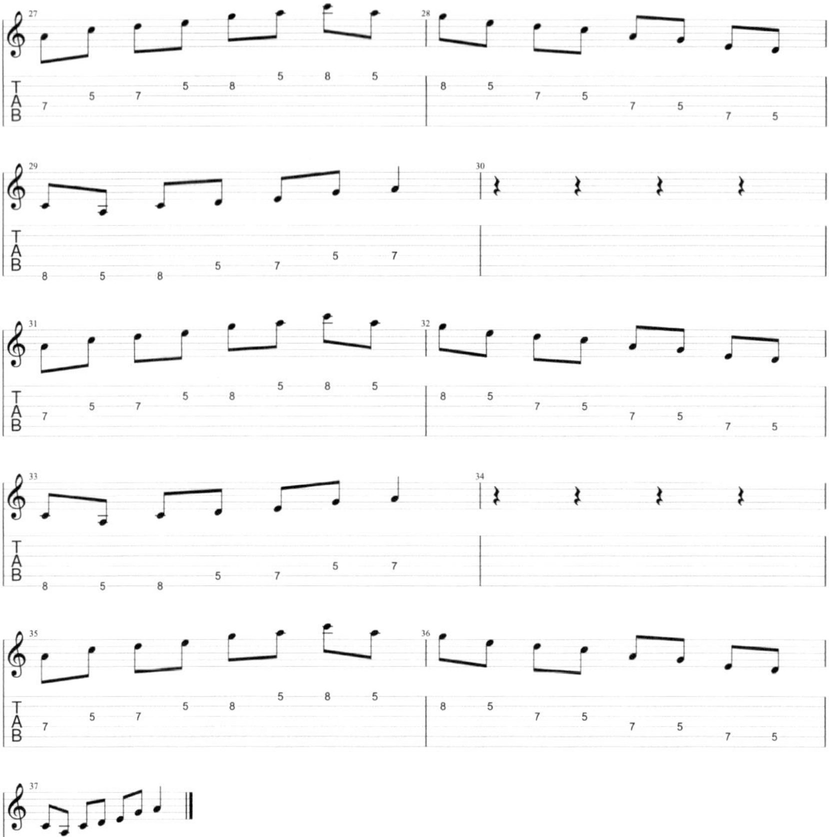

Here we have placed a bar of rests between each repetition. This is a much more sensible way to practice a scale.

If you look at the above tab, you can see that we have placed a bar of rests between each repetition.

This gives you a chance to refocus, and count yourself back in.

This helps ensure that you are playing each repetition nicely in time with the metronome.

If you need to take two bars, or three bars of rest before you come back in, take it. There is no need to rush!

Solution: When practising an exercise to the metronome, make sure you give yourself a little break between repetitions.

This break only needs to be a few seconds, during which you can refocus yourself and come back in.

Mistake 3) Starting to Play Without Listening to 3-4 Clicks or Counting Yourself In

Another common mistake is to put the metronome on and start playing immediately.

When students do this, they never come in on time. It is physically impossible to come in on time if you do this. Let's think about it for a minute.

The metronome is used to measure the passage of time.

To measure the passage of time, you need a starting point and an endpoint.

You need to hear two clicks (at the very least).

If you have only heard one click, it is impossible to know when the second click will be.

And most of us will have to hear 3-4 clicks to get a good feel for the timing.

So by coming in too soon, you are guaranteeing that you will not be playing in time to the metronome.

Solution: When you practice to a metronome, give yourself a 4-beat count in (or whatever is appropriate for the metre you are playing in).

Mistake 4) Not Counting Out Loud to the Metronome

This is a weird one.

If ever there was "one weird secret to improving your guitar playing", this was it.

When I first started teaching, I noticed some students would struggle to play in time to a metronome, even when playing something that was well within their ability level, and at a slow tempo.

For whatever reason, they struggled to count to the metronome, and play the guitar, using only their "internal monologue".

I found that when I made them count out loud to the metronome, their timing improved dramatically, often playing exercises close to perfect, after they had been butchering it just 10 seconds prior.

I use this myself all the time when learning something new.

Sometimes, it can be quite tricky to get the hang of talking out loud and playing the guitar at the same time, but I guarantee, if you put in the time to practice it, it will dramatically improve your timing and accuracy.

Solution: Always count out loud when practising with a metronome. When counting out loud, count confidently, don't whisper or mumble.

Mistake 5) Not Understanding the "Count" of What They Are Playing

Maybe we should have made this an earlier mistake in the list.

A vital part of using a metronome effectively is to understand the count of the music that you are playing.

What we mean by this is, are we counting "1 2 3 4" to the metronome, or "1 + 2 + 3 + 4 +", or "1 e + a 2 e + a 3 e + a 4 e + a", or "1 2 3 2 2 3 3 2 3 4 2 3" or some other method of counting?

Understanding this requires an understanding of rhythm.

Solution: Study the theory of rhythm and learn how to count various rhythms. Make sure you can take any rhythm and dissect it.

Mistake 6) Not Using the Metronome to Count Every Note

This is a mistake I certainly made when I was younger.

I would often use my metronome to count the beat, usually quarter notes.
However, this means that when it comes to playing subdivisions (eighth notes, sixteenths, etc), I was effectively guessing (sometimes more accurately than others!).

For example, if I was playing a section in 16ths and the metronome was counting quarter notes, how would I know if the 16ths that fall between the beat are being played precisely?

I wouldn't.

Solution: Have your metronome count the smallest subdivision that you are playing. If you are playing an exercise that has 16ths, make sure the metronome is counting 16ths. If you are playing something that moves between various subdivisions, consider programming a custom metronome in Guitar Pro / MuseScore / Logic Pro etc.

Mistake 7) Not Counting the Start of the Bar

This is different to Mistake 3, so please read on.
Another common problem is that, after setting the metronome to count the beat or smallest subdivision that they are playing, the student starts playing, gets distracted with a tricky section, and an extra metronome click sneaks past without them realising.

This is especially common when working on a difficult chord change.

Maybe you've experienced this: You're strumming away, perfectly in time to the metronome, the chord change comes up, it's a difficult one, and while you are focussing on moving your fingers to the correct positions, an extra metronome click sneaks past without you realising.

Now, there are various techniques we can use to improve your chord changes, which we'll cover later.

However, there is a nice simple trick we can use with the metronome to help us catch this mistake when it crops up.

Like a lot of things in life, awareness is half the battle.

Solution: Make sure the metronome has a different-sounding "click" on beat 1 of the bar.

After changing the metronome click, you'll know that if you are halfway through a bar and you hear the beat 1 click, you have messed up and you need to go back and figure out what went wrong… and where.

Mistake 8) Not Keeping a Record of Your Metronome Tempos

When practising with a metronome, you will be playing the same exercise for several days, or even weeks, trying to incrementally increase your accuracy… and tempos.

It is well worth keeping a practice log of your tempos and any difficulties you encounter.

At the end of each practice session make a note of the tempo you started at, the tempo you reached, and any notes you want to remind yourself of for your practice session tomorrow.

Maybe you need to make a note that a particular section of an exercise had some string noise that you need to fix or a fret-hand jump that you need to isolate to play correctly.

Solution: Download Bear (https://bear.app/ for Mac OSX) or Evernote (https://evernote.com/) / OneNote (https://www.microsoft.com/en-us/microsoft-365/onenote/digital-note-taking-app for Windows / Mac). Make sure it is ways open when you practice. Read your notes from yesterday before practice, and make some quick notes after you practice.

Here is a screenshot from some of my recent practice notes:

18th August 2021
Maj7 chords strings 5-2.
Exercise 1 Var 2. 90bpm.
Reached 96bpm but was still a bit buzzy in places.

19th August 2021
Maj7 chords strings 5-2.
Exercise 1 Var 2. 95bpm.
Just about reached 104bpm. Get faster tomorrow.

21st August 2021
Maj7 chords strings 5-2.
Exercise 1 Var 2. 100bpm.
106bpm was about comfortable. Get to 110bpm before increasing difficulty.

23rd August 2021
Maj7 chords strings 5-2.
Exercise 1 Var 2. 103bpm.
Had to go down to 95bpm and worked up to 103bpm - I was struggling with this.

My practice notes from working on some chord exercises. I like to use Bear for OSX for keeping notes, not just on guitar practice but everything.

Mistake 9) Using the Wrong Type of Metronome

This mistake is not so common anymore, but some students still make it... I know I did!

There are different types of metronomes, that broadly fall into the four following categories:

- Analogue metronomes. Think of the stick that goes back and forth. A favourite of piano teachers. Avoid using these! They cannot count subdivisions, which is something we require to practice as effectively as possible.
- Digital metronomes. These are usually credit card-sized boxes that you can simply program. You can usually program subdivisions and change the type of click depending on the beat.

- Apps. There are a ton of apps for metronomes for iOS and Android, of varying quality. The best by far is an app called Soundbrenner. This app is free and is highly recommended – I use it quite a lot and recommend it to all my students. We'll look at some examples of how to use Soundbrenner for practising the guitar shortly.
- Custom-programmed metronomes. This is when you make a metronome using a drum track in a program such as Guitar Pro, or Logic Pro. Custom metronomes are fantastic for learning songs. We'll look at some examples of how to set this up later in the article. These are the best types of metronomes we can use. An additional benefit to using a drum metronome is that we can write out the count on the drum part.

I'd recommend learning to program custom metronomes, it is by far the most accurate and useful way to use a metronome.

Mistake 10) Not Taking Breaks Across Large Stretches of Practice

Something that cannot be stated enough, is that your progress on the guitar is dependent on the quality of your practice, not necessarily the amount of time that you practice.

15 minutes of high-quality, focused, distraction-free practice will be 100x more effective than 60 minutes of noodling in front of the TV.

So to get the most from your practice time, it's important to maintain a high level of focus while you are practising.

If you try and practice to a metronome for a long time, you will find you rapidly lose focus after a few minutes.

It is not possible to sit for 60 minutes straight with a metronome, and have the degree of focus at minute 60, that you did at minute 1.

Solution: Set a timer. Practice for 15 minutes, then take a break for 5 minutes. You can always play the same exercise afterwards for another 15 minutes.

You will find that, by doing this, you can maintain your focus much better.

How to Use a Metronome with Specific Exercises

You can check the appendix for specific examples of how to set up a metronome for playing different styles of exercises.

Metronome Expectations

As always, we want to make sure our expectations are in line with reality. When it comes to using a metronome, we will find that the peak tempo we can hit each day will fluctuate - some days it will be higher than others.

Record your peak tempo each day, as previously discussed, and the next day start at a tempo that is lower, maybe 20%-30% lower than your peak, and work your way back towards the peak tempo you hit the previous day.

You might not be able to hit yesterday's peak today… maybe you'll beat yesterday's peak. Either situation is ok, the important thing is that you follow the process. You can also see why it's important to keep a practice log so that you can track these tempos.

You will probably also find that for the first 2-3 weeks, your peak tempo doesn't improve that much. That is because you are still getting the basics of what you are practising into your muscle memory.

I usually find that after 2-3 weeks, my tempos start to rapidly improve. The following graph illustrates this idea:

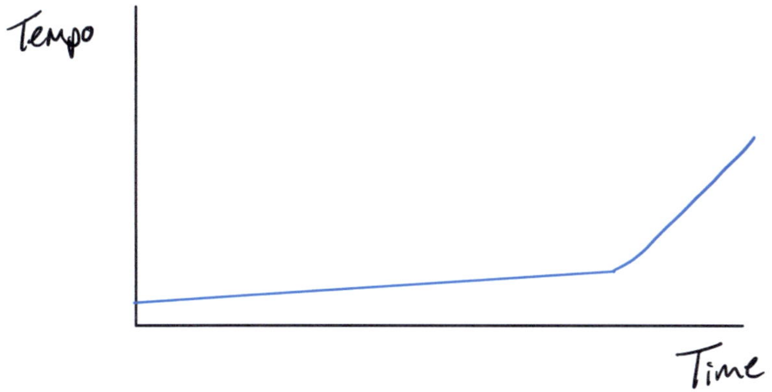

A Selection of Practice Tips and Advice

We have talked extensively about how and why you should use a metronome. Now we are going to look at a collection of other techniques you can use to enhance your guitar practice.

Memorisation

Often when working on an exercise, students will read the exercise as they are playing it. If this is you, you will find it much more effective to memorise what you are working on, rather than trying to read it.

If you are reading an exercise your brain has to deal with visually processing the music on the page, and then it tells your body to play the notes on your guitar.

If you memorise that piece of music, then you can eliminate the mental process of reading the music, which allows you to completely focus on playing the music.

Play Exactly the Same Way Every Time

A common practice mistake students make is to use different fingers when playing a certain section of an exercise. For example, they might play a particular note using the 1st finger, and then the next time they play that note they use their 2nd finger.

This is a huge mistake!

One of the goals of practising is to train our muscle memory to learn specific movements so that we don't have to consciously struggle with every note that we play - we are programming our subconscious on how to play something.

To do this, we have to repeat the exact same motion 100s of times in a row.

When you use random fingers to play an exercise, rather than training that one exercise into your muscle memory, you are training your muscle memory on four... five... nine or even more different exercises simultaneously, which is not very helpful. As you can imagine, this means it takes four... five... nine times as long to learn that piece of music.

This is a big reason why a lot of guitar players struggle to make progress.

So if you would like to learn faster, make a specific choice about what fingers you are going to use and stick to it! If you need to, write the fingers down on the tab you are using.

As a side note, one of the benefits of studying scales is that you get "frameworks" on which fingers to use in different situations. So by studying scales and applying what you learn to other exercises and songs, you will know which fingers you should be using.

What we have discussed about what fingers to use also applies to pick directions - for the same reasons that you should be using the same fingers every time, you should be using the same pick direction every time.

If the piece of music you are working on does not have fingers / pick directions marked on it and you are struggling to remember which fingers / pick directions to use, mark them on your exercise/music.

Reflection

A key part of your practice time is the few minutes after your practice. When you finish a practice session, take a minute to reflect on how the practice session when. Is there anything you can improve about how you approached your practice that you can change tomorrow? Did any problems come up with what you were practising that you need to fix next time you practice? Take a minute to make a note of these thoughts and refer back to them the following day before you practice.

You could keep a specific practice log, or just make some notes in your day planner, the key thing is a simple system that is easy for you to use.

Take Your Time

Everyone is in such a rush. Take your time.

I know that you want to be a better guitar player and that you want to get there as quickly as possible - who doesn't?

But when it comes to working on an exercise, you have to be patient. Often guitar players will play an exercise once and move on.

When you play that exercise, how do you know that you didn't get lucky with that play-through?

You want to make sure that you can play an exercise correctly at least twice, ideally three times in a row before you move on to something new.

I have a nice anecdote about this: When I was in music college, I learned a cool sweep-picking lick. I went to a rehearsal and showed my friend. He then asked me to play it a second time and a big string of garbage came out of my guitar. What I had "learned" was cool, but I wasn't yet able to use it in musical situations as part of my guitar playing.

He told me "If you can't play it twice, you can't play it" and that stuck with me.

That was also the last time I made that practice mistake.

If you are practising something that requires a deep focus on muscle memory, then you may want to continue practising an exercise that you "can do" for a week before increasing the tempo / moving on to something new. This goes back to the levels of learning we covered earlier, with conscious/subconscious levels.

Once you have "got" something, you are using your conscious mind to play the technique. However, we want these techniques to be part of our subconscious mind. Repeatedly practising a conscious-level technique will, over time, push that technique down into your subconscious.

Muscle Tension

When you are a beginner, you will find learning guitar uncomfortable. Short of ballet dancing, learning guitar is probably one of the most uncomfortable things you can do with your body - you have to position yourself in a very unsymmetrical position and focus on very fine motor skills.

When we are learning guitar, one element that we are learning is how to use certain muscle groups in certain ways - which is something you can say of any skill.

You will find that you are unable to control your muscles in the way you want, and you will almost certainly find that your muscles do odd things that you don't want them to do.

A lot of students find that when concentrating, they introduce additional muscle tension into their bodies. A good example of this is shoulder tension - when approaching a section of music a student knows they struggle with, they will tense their shoulders and hunch their back over the guitar, sometimes so much so that it is obvious to anyone watching.

Next time you are practising a piece of music that is difficult, stop and ask yourself if you are feeling tenser than you need to be.

Another way muscle tension is introduced is "just because", which is where you needlessly tense up anytime you are playing the guitar. This could be any muscle group from your feet and legs to even your tongue! Again, next time you sit down with your guitar, ask yourself if you are needlessly tensing up muscle groups that do not need to be tense.

How Much Muscle Tension Should You Use?

Just enough, and no more! You need to use enough tension to ensure the notes ring out correctly, and no more than that. Additional tension is not only wasted energy but something that will inhibit your playing.

Sympathetic Muscle Tension

This is when a muscle group tenses in reaction to a different muscle group being used. For example, let's say you are tremolo picking a series of notes. Your pick hand will tense up, which is necessary to perform the technique correctly, but often students find that their fret hand will also tense up.

Now, the fretting hand does not need to hold down the strings any harder than normal for the picking hand to play them, so this additional muscle tension is completely unnecessary.

If you find yourself doing this, you will want to train yourself to stop doing it. Take your guitar and play a single note repeatedly. Vary the tension in your pick hand while trying to keep your fret hand at the same consistent level of tension.

This will take a bit of trial and error to get right, but you will find that after a bit of practice, maybe 5-10minutes a day, your body starts to "figure it out" and you will relax a bit more when playing.

Reduce Muscle Tension With Good Posture

A lot of muscle tension problems can be solved by improving your posture. There is an appendix at the end with plenty of photographs to demonstrate good posture.

Dealing With Frustration

When working on a difficult piece of music that is slightly beyond your ability, it is natural to become frustrated with it. When this happens it is important to relax before continuing. Take a 3 minute break. Make a cup of tea, and go outside for a few minutes.

When frustrated, we often start to tense up our body, which will make the piece that we are working on even harder to play.

The Myth of Perfection

Perfection is a goal that we will never reach. This isn't to say we shouldn't aim for it, but if we use it as a goal we will never be happy - or learn anything new!

It can be tempting to say that you will only move on to the next exercise once you have the current exercise perfect, but this is a trap. Your current exercise will never be perfect, you will never move to the next exercise and you will never progress.

Instead, aim to get what you are working on 80%-90% correct and then move on to the next exercise. You will often find that by doing this, when you revisit an only exercise that last 10-20% has magically developed.

The reason for doing this is that when we aim for perfection, the 80/20 rule starts to work against us.

The 80/20 rule states that it takes 20% of the effort to get 80% of the results. Or to put it another way, 80% of the effort only generates 20% of the results.

Getting 80% of the results and moving on is a much more effective way to progress quickly than spending all your time getting the last little bit right.

The exception to this is if you are practising for a performance or recording session. In that case, you would want to make sure you have all the little detail worked out, which will take enormous amounts of time. So make sure you plan for the extra time that you will need!

Problem Solving Strategies

When practising, you are going to come across sections of music and exercises that you struggle with, and it's important that you have a selection of tools to tackle those problems as they arise.

The general approach to solving any problem with your guitar playing is as follows:

1. Figure out exactly what the problem is
2. Isolate the problem
3. Practice that specific thing until you get it right
4. Slowly re-integrate back into the piece (start at a slow tempo and work your way up).

When figuring out the problem, you have to be specific. Really specific. "I can't play this" is not specific. "I can't play the chord change" is better. "I can't move from Em to G" is better. "When moving from Em to G, my first finger on my left hand goes to the wrong string" is best - this gives you the information you need to fix the problem.

You can now focus on moving that first finger correctly and fixing your problem.

So when you are trying to diagnose your guitar-playing problems, take a minute to think through what is going on and be as specific as possible.

Sometimes when playing, it can be difficult to figure out what our hands are doing as we are so focused on playing. If this is the case, video yourself on your phone and watch the video back and figure out what it is you are doing.

Next, we'll look at some specific strategies that you can use to fix the problems that you are having.

Isolation

Let's say you are working on a song that is 5 minutes long. Most guitar players tend to practice songs by playing through them from start to finish. Let's also say that there is a chord change you struggling with towards the end of the song.

A lot of players will practice by playing through the song, hitting the difficult chord change, screwing up and going back to the start for a second attempt.

Earlier in the book, we talked about the distinction between practising and playing. In this case, you are spending most of your practice time playing the guitar, and not practising. 95% of the song is within your ability, it is only the 5%, that chord change at the end, that needs to be practised.

So why not spend all the practice time practising the hard stuff?

A more efficient way to practice would be to take the chord change at the end and set up a loop using Guitar Pro (or your DAW), to practice that specific part of the song that you are struggling with.

Let's also say that you have 30 minutes to practice a day. In 30 minutes, the 5-minute song can be played 6 times. That's not very many times… it's going to take a while to get that last chord change correct if you can only play it 6 times!

The problematic chord change is in a 15-second section of music.

If you were to isolate and practice the difficult chord change, you could practice that 120 times in 30 minutes.

120 repetitions versus 6 repetitions...

So in this example, by practising using isolation, you will progress 120 times faster than if you play the song all the way through from start to finish!

This isn't to say that you should never play songs from start to finish, you should and doing so is important to practice - especially if you are rehearsing for a gig! But when there is something you are struggling with, isolate it and work intensely on it to solve it, then go back to playing the song all the way through.

Isolation to the Ridiculous

When practising, you may find that your hands do weird things from time to time. When you find this happening, you can take the concept of isolation to the extreme, and isolate the specific hand that is causing the problem.

For example, if your left hand is doing something weird, take the motion that you are trying to achieve and practice moving your left hand that way. Don't worry about the right hand, put it down by your side so that it doesn't distract you. Just focus on moving your left hand correctly. You will find that after 5-10 minutes you have solved the problem.

If you have a problem with your right hand, for example trying a complex string skipping pattern, then you can do exactly the same thing. Put your left hand down by your side and practice moving the right hand correctly, just playing through open strings.

You can take this even further and apply it to individual finer movements that are proving problematic.

Synchronisation

This technique applies specifically to scale-based problems you may be having. When we start to push the limits of how fast we can play with scale-based exercises, the two hands often start to go out of sync with each other.

We can improve that by playing each note in the exercise twice.

As an example, let's say you were working on the following melody:

When we double up each note, we get:

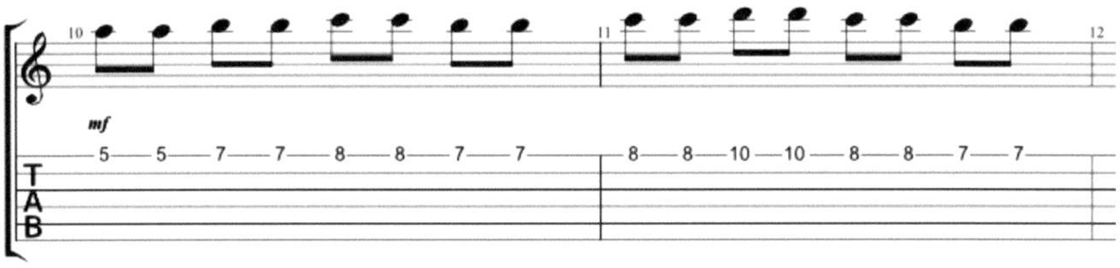

Note that we are keeping the same note value as the original (in this case, everything is being played with eighth notes). We would be using alternate picking in this case.

By playing the exercise like this, we force our hands to move at different rates - in the original exercise we pick eighth notes and our fret hand also changes with eighth notes. In the second exercise, our pick hand is still playing eighth notes, but now the fretting hand is moving at a quarter-note speed.

You will find playing the exercise this way does wonders for your synchronisation and will help you push the original exercise to higher tempos while being more accurate.

Practising Chord Changes

I thought I would add this section as something a lot of guitar players struggle with is improving their chord changes.

They either can't change fast enough, or their fingers can't find the right place on the neck… or their fingers just do weird stuff!

So here are some of my best tips for improving your chord changes on guitar:

Grip and Release

This is a simple and highly effective exercise.

Hold the chord down, really, really hard.

You should be holding it down so hard that the tips of your fingernails turn yellow.

Hold the chord down like this for 6-8 seconds, then relax. When you relax, completely relax your arm and hand down by your side.

When telling students to relax their arm completely, I often see them relax their hand partially… which is not what I asked them to do!

So make sure that you relax your arm completely.

You must relax your arm, as you are introducing massive amounts of tension into your arm, and that needs to be dissipated.

Repeat the exercise 5-6 times for each chord that you are working on.

You will find that this exercise helps your fingers “find” the chord faster.

Slow Changes

When it comes to moving your hand to a new chord, there are two stages:
1. Moving the hand so that the hand is roughly over the correct frets.
2. Move your fingers to the right strings/frets.

Step 1 is quite easy - moving your arm horizontally up or down a few frets on the guitar doesn’t take any skill or thought.

Step 2 is a lot trickier. You have to use precise motor skills to hold down the correct chord.

Your ability to execute step 1 quickly will often far exceed your ability to execute step 2 quickly.

Often, a student will move their hand quickly to the right position, then their fingers will “flail” around as they try to hold down the chord as quickly as they moved their hand… which they cannot do.

I like to call this effect “Bambi on ice”, as their fingers look like a baby deer trying to stand whilst walking on ice!

But in all seriousness, this creates a problem - every time you move your hand this way, you are practising “wiggling” your fingers… you are not practising holding down the chord correctly.

You need to practice moving your fingers directly to where they need to go, not going all over the neck before they find the right spot.

To fix this, take your hand off the guitar, relax it by your side, then bring your hand back to the neck, SLOWLY.

Make sure each finger moves directly to where it needs to go, to hold down the chord that you are learning.

You should not be re-arranging your fingers and they should not be wiggling or dancing over the strings - if they do any of these things, you are moving too fast and you must slow down.

You may be surprised at just how slowly you need to move your fingers to do this correctly, but take the time.

The secret to learning guitar quickly is to practice things slowly - practising too fast is not practising at all, it's just wasting time.

You can also apply this exercise to moving between two chords.

Right Hand Always in Time

We often struggle when practising a new chord change, because it's new. This is normal and to be expected.

So when practising, we'll be playing through a few chords, we get to the one that we are struggling with and we can't quite play it in time - every time we get to that chord it takes us a little longer to find it than the other chords that we are playing.

We move our fret hand to the correct position, it takes us a little longer to find that position, and then our strumming hand finally strums the strings - much later than we wanted to.

Every time we do this we are practising playing out of time - we are practising leaving extra time for this particular chord!

Here's how we fix that: Play through the chord progression using a metronome, and keep the strumming hand perfectly in time, EVEN IF the left hand can't find the chord.

This will be quite difficult, as you have been practising playing the chord out of time for so long.

And when you do this, you will find that you make a horrible sound from your guitar.

And when you do it the next time, you will find that you still make a horrible sound from your guitar.

But if persist, you will find that after 10-15 repetitions/attempts, your chord change starts to feel a bit smoother.

If it doesn't start feeling better after 10-15 repetitions, then slow down the metronome and isolate the chord change (see the previous section on isolation).

This is a weird way to practice, but it is very effective.

Think Ahead

When you start to become a bit more advance at guitar, you have to start moving and thinking your body and mind out of time with the music, to be able to play in time.

This is a good example of that idea.

When you are holding down a particular chord, you are holding down that particular chord.

Obvious, right?

This means that you do not need to be thinking about that chord.

This means that you can be thinking about the next chord that you want to play.

While holding down any particular chord, have your brain think ahead about what the next chord will be - try and visualise it in your mind and you will find your fingers can find it a little easier.

Look Where You Want to Play

In addition to thinking about the chord you want to play, physically look at where you want your hand to be.

Often, new guitar players will only look at where they want to move their hand when it's time to play that chord, or even worse, they'll be staring off into space while practising.

This means that the beat comes around, they move their head to look at where they want to play the next chord, and then they move their hands to play the chord.

By the time the beat has come around, it is already too late. Moving your head creates a split second that is lost before you can start moving your hand.

In the previous idea, we talked about thinking ahead of time, you also want to look ahead of time.

While playing a particular chord, you don't need to look at it - so physically move your head and look at where the next chord will go.

This will save you a lot of time and help you play those chords more accurately.

This does not apply to just chord changes, but everything you want to do on guitar - physically look ahead before you need to and you'll find your playing improves.

Rubber Band Arm

This is a killer problem for getting your chords in time.

Often, a student will strum a chord, then their arm will "rest" between the high string and the floor. They wait for the beat to come around, hold down the next chord, and then bring their arm up to the bass strings so that they can then strum the chord.

The act of bringing the arm up creates a small delay between when they want to play the chord and when they can play the chord, and that small delay often throws out their timing.

This is easy to fix - after strumming a chord, bring the arm back up to the bass strings automatically.

Pretend that your arm has a giant rubber band attached, from your wrist to your neck, and every time you strum down, bring the arm back up so that it is ready and waiting for the next chord.

This will save you a lot of time and make your strumming much better!

Anticipate the Beat

This is the final problem that students face when strumming - anticipating the beat.

Often, especially at the early stages, a student will "wait" for the click on the metronome to sound before they then play.

Of course, by the time you have heard the metronome, it is too late to play in time with the metronome.

The click must be anticipated - at first, you will be effectively guessing when the click is going to sound, but with practice, you will quickly improve and develop the skill to be able to anticipate the metronome.

The metronome must always be anticipated, and never waited for.

Set Your Practice for What You Are Practising For

Recently, I played a couple of concerts with a cellist. I had written an album of duets for electric guitar and cello, and the cellist and I performed them at a couple of concerts.

However, the first gig did not go so well for me. While I had practised plenty, I found it much harder than I should have. This was partially down to nerves, but there was something else going on.

After the gig, I tried to figure out what had made the performance so challenging. Eventually, I figured it out - I had been practising listening to a metronome playing over the cello parts, and without that metronome, I had to listen to the cello to stay in time, something that I had not practised doing before which I found incredibly taxing mentally.

To put it another way, I had practised focussing my listening on the metronome, not the cellist. Without the metronome, I had to focus on the cellist to stay in time.

There was a two-week gap before the next gig, so I turned off the metronome, learned the cello score in-depth and figured out which parts of the cello melody started each bar and my parts overlapped with so that I could stay in time.

I practised listening to the cellist while playing my parts on top (this is another great advantage of using a DAW to practice, which we'll go over later).

The second gig went much better.

The moral of the story here is that you have to practice for the conditions that you are going to be playing in.

Now, this isn't to say "don't use a metronome", metronomes are a vital part of practice and should be an early step in learning whatever piece of music you are playing.

But once you can play in time with a metronome, you have to learn to play in time with whatever instruments you will be playing with - for most of the people reading this, that will be a drum kit.

This isn't training your ability to stay in time, but it is training your ability to listen to specific instruments while playing.

If possible, get the drummer in your band to write out their parts in MIDI, then you can import the MIDI into your DAW, mockup some drums and learn how the drums work with your guitar parts. Then you will always have rock-solid timing when playing with your band.

Practising for Speed

We previously discussed how when it comes to practice, you want to practice playing accurately and that speed will naturally develop from accuracy. But there are a few things we can do to push things along faster.

Practice Technique Exercises on Acoustic Guitar

Spend a few minutes when you are working on your technique exercises playing them on an acoustic guitar. Acoustic guitar strings, compared to electric guitar strings, are big and heavy.

After playing the acoustic for a few minutes, switch back to electric. You will find that your fingers feel a lot "lighter" on the strings and will fly over the fretboard.

Time Expectations for Developing Speed

Developing speed takes time. Michael Angelo Batio (worth a listen if you've never heard of him) has previously said that he spent two hours a day just working on his technique for two years to take it to the insane levels he reached.

Hitting those high levels of technique takes a minimum of practising three hours a day. If you are going to commit to an intensive training program with this much practice, bear in mind everything we discussed earlier about warning signs of injury, building up your practice over time and keeping a healthy body.

How to Practice Without a Guitar

We don't always have a guitar to hand, so what can we do to practice in those situations?

There are a few things that we can do:

- Visualisation
- Mental practice
- Picking practice
- Composing
- Reading

Visualisation

When it comes to playing scales and chords on the guitar, we have to mentally recall the shape/pattern that we want to use, then we create that pattern on the guitar. If we are away from the guitar, we can practice recalling these shapes in our mind. This can be a highly effective way to improve your ability to remember shapes.

A while ago, a student of mine went on a cycling holiday with her partner. There were some challenging climbs on their route, and during those climbs, she would picture in her mind where different arpeggio shapes are on the guitar.

She came back from that holiday with excellent arpeggio recall - you could give her a chord progression and she would be able to play it as arpeggios on the spot.

While I wouldn't recommend you do this while you're driving or doing some complex skill where you have to focus if you are on the bus with a few minutes to kill this is a great way to make that time productive.

Mental Practice

Several studies have shown that practising in your mind, where you picture yourself practising, in the short term, is just as effective as actually practising with an instrument.

So when you are away from your guitar, you can shut your eyes and focus, and picture yourself playing a piece of music. This is effective for about a week, after which real practice is more beneficial.

Another way you can practice in your mind is to go over music theory concepts. You can run through the notes in a scale, scale harmonisations, notes in a chord, pivot chords for modulation; just about any music theory concept you can think of you can run through in your mind (or on paper).

Picking Practice

This works well if you wear jeans. Your jeans have a chunky seam down the side of the leg. You can use this seam to simulate a string. Take your pick, use a metronome on your phone that you can listen to with headphones and using your pick, pick a rhythm against the seam of your jeans in time with the metronome.

This is an incredibly effective way to focus on a particular rhythm that you may be struggling with. If you are sitting on the train for 20 minutes, that's 20 minutes of intensive rhythm practice you can do.

If you are doing that once a day, Monday to Friday, that comes to 86.67 HOURS of extra rhythm practice a year.

These little things can add up when you take a long-term view of your playing.

Compose

This one may be a little harder depending on your environment, but is a great use of time. You can use a laptop, tablet or paper and compose some music. Write a chord progression, a prelude, a rondo, a sonata or some other form. Write a song. Work on lyrics for a song.

Composing away from the guitar can be a great way to unlock creative ideas that you wouldn't have had if you were composing on guitar. Understanding some music theory is a real help when doing this, as you won't rely on your improvisation skills to compose.

Reading

Last but certainly not least, if you are away from your guitar you can read a book. There are a lot of great music theory books that you can read that will give you a new insight into music and how it works.

You can take a book of blank music notation and a pencil and work through problems.

When travelling to Spain a couple of years ago, I would take some blank notation and a theory book and work on counterpoint problems in the airport lounge and on the plane. It was a very productive flight!

I'll include a list of music theory books I recommend in the appendix.

How to Deal with Bad Practice Days

Sometimes, things are just not working on the guitar. We can't focus, can't play like normal… we're just having a bit of an off day.

On these days, try and find something that you can do. Maybe it's something like jamming along to a backing track. Or practice a simple scale much slower than usual. Or taking some normal aspect of your practice routine and just doing 10 minutes on it before calling it quits.

Find something that you can do, so that you avoid days where you don't do anything. If you allow yourself days to do nothing (aside from your rest day), then you will find these days become more frequent.

If you get yourself doing something, even if it isn't for long, you will find you have fewer unproductive days and also develop your work ethic nicely.

Section 3: Studying

Towards the start of this book, we discussed how creativity can be seen as taking different concepts and mixing them. So it stands to reason that the more concepts you know and truly understand, the more ideas you will be able to experiment with and try out, hence, the more creative you will become.

In this section we are going to go over some approaches you can take to studying, to help you learn more effectively. Learning effectively is key to creativity.

Some Problems Take a Long Time to Solve

Albert Einstein is famous for his theory of Special Relativity, and later, General Relativity. Archimedes is famous for his theory on buoyancy.

When we hear the stories of great thinkers and their discoveries, we are often told of the breakthrough moment when the pieces finally fell into place and they figured out the problem.

What we are rarely told is the amount of thinking that happened before that moment, thinking time that is often measured in months or even years.

Einstein spent 10 years thinking over the problems around special relativity before he had a breakthrough that enabled him to publish his groundbreaking theory.

When considering a problem, people are often quick to dismiss their ability to solve the problem (or understand the lesson) if they are unable to instantly grasp it. Sometimes problems need a little time to solve - this is completely normal, but something that seems to have been "forgotten".

Next time you are stuck with a problem you can't figure out, sit for five minutes and try and crack it. When you are working on some music theory concept you are struggling with, give yourself a few days to work through it.

Some more complex theories/topics may take you months to work through… or even years. That's ok. The important thing is that you:

1. Stick at it

2. Progress a little more than you did last week

Laying Out Your Ideas

One of the biggest roadblocks people face in solving problems in music is understanding the information. This applies to everything from writing chord progressions to composing a symphony.

Often people try and do things in their head, but there is too much to consider and they get confused and make mistakes. Lay out the relevant pieces of information on paper. This lets you consider things more easily.

When laying things out on paper, make sure you do so in a way that makes sense. Before you consider the problem, consider the best way to organise solving the problem.

Figuring out how to lay out the information clearly is a problem itself that needs to be solved, and figuring this out might take a few attempts!

I usually find with music theory problems, once you lay out the information properly on paper, the solution becomes obvious.

Annotated scores or diagrammatic blocks are usually helpful ways to lay out ideas. Tables can be useful when working with chords.

Prose is almost certainly the wrong way to lay out a music theory problem (unless you sketching plot ideas for a concept album/ libretto).

To summarise, problem-solving has three steps:

1. Consider the best way to approach solving the problem.

2. Lay that out on paper.

3. Solve the problem.

Where to Learn From

We live in an age with countless sources of information at our fingertips. The downside is that this can be overwhelming - with so many sources of information available, where should you learn from?

There are three main sources I am going to recommend:

- Textbooks
- Courses
- Teachers
- Playing in a band/duo/ensemble etc

Let's discuss a little bit about the "concept" of learning, then we will come back to these sources and others.

We mentioned towards the start of this book that concepts exist in an interconnected hierarchy. Some concepts are simpler than others. To understand complex concepts, we must first understand the simpler concepts on which they rely.

We can think of a song as being a complex concept, relying on the concepts of harmony, melody, structure, rhythm and texture. We can think of harmony as a complex concept, relying on the simpler concepts of intervals and scales.

When learning any subject, especially something as complex as music, we want to move from lower-level concepts to higher-level concepts. We need to understand how these concepts are structured vertically, and also how they are interconnected to each other.

Good textbooks, courses and teachers achieve this; by giving clear structure to the ideas that they are presenting.

You can also see why things such as YouTube and magazines are not so effective for proper learning. The lessons are not structured.

This isn't to say that you shouldn't use things like YouTube and magazines, they are a great way to supplement your learning, providing material around the subject you are studying, but I would strongly advise against using them as your main source.

Additionally, while there is a wealth of information on YouTube, it rarely goes into the depth that a textbook/teacher will go into.

How to Find Good Books / Courses / Teachers

Now that we know what type of material we want to look for, we need to narrow it down. First, how can you tell if something is relevant to what you are wanting to study, and second, how can we tell if it is any good?

Reviews are can be helpful. If you are looking at a teacher or a course, you can look at the musical output of that teacher/course creator - do you like their records and the music that they have released? Do you like their playing?

When it comes to courses, they often have testimonials on the sales page/website. Try and find the people that gave the testimonial and ask them what they really think - testimonials are great, but they are sometimes taken out of context.

When looking at testimonials, make sure that the testimonial aligns with the outcome that you want. For example, if you are looking at a course on how to write melodies, and all the testimonials say things like "I really enjoyed this course", and "This is a great course"; then maybe that course isn't so good. If the testimonials include MP3s of the songs that the people who took the course wrote, then there is a better chance the course will be helpful. If the reviews say something like "I went from struggling to compose to being able to easily write new melodies", then there is a better chance the course will be useful.

Getting opinions from others in Facebook groups and Reddit groups can also be useful. A couple of years ago I was trying to find a music theory textbook that would explain classical form and had some very helpful advice from Reddit groups.

It might inevitably take a few tries to find what you are looking for. You may have to try out a few different teachers, courses or books before you find one that clicks with you. You may find you want to study with multiple sources at once. When trying a source out, try and stick to it for at least a month before deciding if it is working for you (unless it is truly horrific).

Warning Signs of Bad Teachers

Having said that, there are a lot of bad teachers out there. Here are a few signs you can use to filter out bad teachers and find a good teacher when you are searching:

- You want a teacher that asks you about your specific goals.
- Your teacher should not swear in your initial communications.
- What do their previous students say about them?
- Do you leave their lessons feeling like you have learned something or progressed?
- Do they spend lessons talking about their life, or teaching you?
- If you make a serious effort but do not get the results, do they blame you?

Those are the warning signs of a bad teacher. The major warning sign of an inexperienced teacher is that they will give you too much to do each lesson - every lesson will be new material and you don't have enough time to practice the previous material properly (even if you are practising a reasonable amount each day). They might be a good teacher but are overestimating how much new material you need - if you think they are worth continuing with then ask them to reign things back a bit.

An extreme and slightly dark side to bad teachers is that some cultivate a cult-like attitude around them - yes, guitar cults do exist!

This is usually done as a marketing ploy, as those in a cult do not question it and will keep paying to be a member.

You can spot these cults by:

- Looking at what the members say. Are they all repeating buzzwords without really understanding or questioning those ideas?
- What results are they getting? Are they all mediocre guitar players talking about the secrets to playing well?
- Do they posture to have "insider knowledge" or "secrets" that no one else does?
- Does leaving the cult have negative consequences - no longer being able to talk to your former friends?
- Do they encourage you to stop talking to your friends?

Fortunately, these are rare, but they are out there and it's worth knowing how to spot the warning signs.

The Benefits of Playing in a Band

I'll include bands/duos/ensembles etc under this playing with other people. (FYI an ensemble is just a group of musicians playing together).

Playing in a band is a "real world" test of your musical abilities and if there are any holes or weaknesses, they will very quickly be exposed. It is also an incredibly fun thing to do!

Being in a band will force you to listen to all the other instruments that are playing and make sure that you know the songs you are playing inside out.

You will also find it's an opportunity to work on your communication skills, leadership skills and management skills; getting a band to the level where you are playing small pub shows takes work in all these areas.

If you look at the biographies of great guitar players, it is quite common that they started playing in bands that performed very early.

If you are struggling to find other people to form a band with, you can try:

- Local Facebook groups.
- Ask your teacher.
- Phone local teachers of other instruments and ask if any of their students want to form a band.
- Internet websites for finding band members.
- Ask online communities you are part of.
- University societies can be a good way to meet people if you are a student.
- Ask your friends if they know anyone.

There is a lot that can go into a band that is outside the scope of this book, but I may write an article or two about it on the study guitar blog.

The Fifth Source of Information: Analysis

When it comes to learning how to be creative, it is vital to learn from the masters. Take your favourite songs and pieces of music and analyse how they have been put together.

There are seven elements of music, and by analysing each element you will understand how the piece of music works the way it does. These seven elements are:

- Harmony
- Melody
- Form
- Dynamics
- Texture
- Rhythm

• Timbre

You will have to learn a lot of theory to be able to analyse pieces to a degree of detail where you can learn something from them - you will have to study each element of music individually. Having a teacher walk you through some pieces to analyse would be helpful.

You can also consider finding a teacher to specifically help you do musical analysis.

When doing analysis, you will start by "cataloguing" the different elements of music that are being used. To go back to an earlier section, we could consider this the "perceptual" level of understanding the music (which isn't to say this is easy, it can be difficult to figure out what is going on).

After figuring out "what" is being done, you want to think about how that creates the musical effect that it does. Exactly what about the music do you like? Exactly what elements of music are being used to create that effect?

In the earlier section on learning guitar, we talked about being specific when it came down to problem-shooting your technique. Be specific here too.

Is there a specific emotion or feeling that you like at a specific point in the song? What specific elements of music are creating that? The harmony? The rhythm? The ornamentation on the guitar? Something else? Take the time to sit down and figure it out.

Information and Entertainment

Sometimes students want to be more productive with their studying, but take a very unproductive approach to it. It's usually from confusing entertainment with education.

Things like guitar magazines and YouTube videos (aside from a few select channels) usually fall under entertainment.

Textbooks, courses and work from a teacher are education.

Sometimes people want to feel like they are "doing more" for their education by watching loads of videos about guitar playing on YouTube or reading guitar magazines. While you may pick up the odd tip here and there, you are not achieving anything. In the business world, this is called "Action Faking".

You get the feeling that you are doing something productive, but really you have achieved as much as if you had watched a movie (at least watching a movie would be relaxing!).

If you instead took that time to practice, read a music theory textbook, or even read the manual for the recording program or other software you use, you would have improved and learned something.

Now I'm not saying that you should completely remove entertainment from your life, entertainment is great for relaxing, which is an important part of the day. But you may find there are ways you can easily fit something more productive into your day.

And don't cut into your practice under the pretence that you are doing something useful when you are entertaining yourself. Practice time is for practice time, not YouTube and magazines!

Conferences and Live Events

This could range from a BBQ/garden party to a full 10-day in-person course. If you are taking lessons with a teacher, then you may find they do events where students can meet each other. With my students, we would occasionally have a dinner out at a local pub, BBQ or play at the local open mic night.

Some international teachers or course creators may offer live events. I would recommend trying these out if you can. I've been on a few and they have always been a great experience and you often make friends there, some of whom will be friends for life.

If nothing else, you get a total immersion in your interest, and you get to be around people trying things out that you can learn from. You will find people that can give you recommendations and advice, people you can collaborate with, play gigs with, or just hang out and have fun.

In addition (or instead of) attending a conference on guitar/ composition, you can always find conferences and events for your other interests. I recently attended a philosophy conference in London, UK where I met a lot of interesting people, a few of whom I have kept in contact with since.

People who attend conferences tend to be people who are doing things with their lives. If you give it a chance and introduce yourself to as many people as you can, you are bound to find a few people that you click with.

When it comes to “success” having a “network” (which is a fancy way of saying ‘friends that are competent at what they do’) can make your life a LOT easier. Conferences and live events are great ways to find those people.

Be Ruthless in Your Pursuit of Understanding

How hard do you push yourself when learning something new? There are several levels of understanding that students can take:

1. Cursory reading of the material
2. Being able to recite key terms and definitions
3. Replicating examples
4. Being able to explain key terms and definition
5. Replicating examples in different keys
6. Replicating examples in different contexts

Let’s illustrate these ideas with an example. Let’s say we are learning about composition and have just read about passing tones.

At Level 1, we read about passing tones and that is it. We might be able to tell someone that we read about passing tones at the weekend, but we couldn't say much more than reciting the name "passing tone" to someone.

At Level 2 we have pushed the boat out a little further and have memorised key definitions. We can recite that a passing tone is when "We have two chord tones a third apart, and add in the note in-between." In our notes, we would have an annotated score to demonstrate the idea.

Level 3 is quite similar to Level 2, but we can replicate the notation example of how a passing tone works. We'll discuss this a bit more later, but notation examples are much more effective at reminding you how a music theory concept works than a sentence.

At Level 4 we can re-word the definition in a few different ways. This is a good way to start to test your understanding as your brain now has to work conceptually. At Levels 1 and 2 you are merely reciting words and you are not doing much better than a parrot. By re-wording definitions you have to consider what the words mean, create a mental model of what the concepts that words are representing and figure out a new way to explain the key elements of that model to someone.

At Level 5 we start to understand how passing tones work. We can take an example of a passing tone over an A minor harmony and create an example over an E major harmony that uses a passing tone.

At Level 6 we can say that we really understand what is going on, being able to take the concept of passing tones and apply them in different contexts. Maybe we apply it to compose a melody for a singer, to bending notes on electric guitar, or composing a 4 part model for orchestra.

Perceptual and Conceptual Levels of Understanding

We could break the 6 levels of understanding into two main categories:

- Perceptual
- Conceptual

At the perceptual level, we are in "monkey see monkey do" mode. Unfortunately, a lot of us are programmed to think this way at school, where we are taught that learning consists of memorising and repeating endless lists of random facts.

The conceptual level of thinking is where we start to become creative.

Good teachers and textbooks will push you to think conceptually about the material that you are covering. The point of exercises in textbooks and assignments from teachers is to push your understanding to more conceptual levels.

It's important to note that thinking this way is a process, and more often than not we have to move through the levels - we are going to struggle to think conceptually if we can't replicate examples or give a simple definition. This process also takes time - when working on a topic, it may take several lessons or longer to move you from perceptual to conceptual levels of understanding.

Perceptual

- Level 1 - Simply reading
- Level 2 - Reciting key terms
- Level 3 - Replicating examples

Conceptual

- Level 4 - Explaining key terms
- Level 5 - Changing key of examples
- Level 6 - Change context of examples

When studying you want to bear these levels in mind and make sure that you are working through them.

Test yourself as you go.

Sometimes students "read the words on the page" and do not consider the meaning of those words. When reading a textbook, ask yourself "So what? What does this paragraph mean?". Don't settle for looking at words on a page, challenge your understanding as you go.

Those Who Understand, Create

It's fine to read through a music theory or composition concept and think "Sure, I understand this", it's another to take that idea and use it to create a short piece of music. When we talked about the 6 levels of understanding, at Level 6 we talked about changing the context of the concept we are studying, or to put it another way, composing a short piece of music using that idea.

Creation is the litmus test for understanding.

Creation is the purpose of studying in the first place, there is no point in studying if you are not going to apply it to something and use that knowledge to create.

In addition to creation being the purpose of studying, it is also a fantastic way to study. By taking an idea that you are learning and trying to compose with it (this composition may only be two bars long, or a whole sonata depending on the topic you are studying), you will very quickly expose any holes in your knowledge that you need to then solve.

These holes could be caused by not understanding the material properly, or it could be a flaw with the material that you are studying - not all courses and textbooks are perfect! If you have a teacher, keep track of these questions throughout the week in a notebook or computer file and ask them at the next lesson (I have taught several lessons where we just went through student questions).

If you don't have a teacher, then you may need to consult other textbooks or sources to find the answers that you are looking for. You can always try reaching out to the course creator or book author, a lot of people are surprisingly reachable via email. The worst that they will do is not reply, so it doesn't hurt to reach out and ask a question or two.

So as soon as you learn a new idea, find a way to use it and try it out. You will find you learn a lot faster and more thoroughly by doing this.

How to Learn Any Song

This applies to songs, exercises, your compositions; anything where you have more than a few bars of music to work through. There are several ways to approach learning a piece of music, most of which are incredibly inefficient.

One way is to work through the song from the start. Every time you make a mistake, go back to the start of the song. This is very inefficient, as you spend a lot of time playing through bits you already know rather than working on the bits that need work. This is probably the most common approach.

A better way to approach learning a song is as follows. Start with bar 1. Apply the following process:

1. Figure out where the frets/notes are on the guitar and what fingers you are going to use to play those notes.
2. Annotate your music with the fingers if you need a reminder (this is a very useful tip when starting with a piece!)
3. Play through a few times making sure that you play it the same way every time using the fingers you previously specified. Do this SLOWLY, so that you don't make too many mistakes - many students rush this phase.
4. Work out the rhythm of the piece. You may want to write this under the music.
5. Play through that bar slowly, counting the rhythm out loud - counting out loud is important, if you count in your head you will make mistakes.
6. Take your metronome, at a slow tempo and clap the rhythm, counting out loud to the metronome.
7. Take your guitar and play along to the metronome, counting out loud.
8. Once you can play the bar 3 times in a row (with a break between each repetition), learn the next bar.

This process will help you learn anything on guitar. It's helpful if you memorise what you are working on.

In terms of how you work through the song, use the following approach:

1. Learn bar 1.
2. Learn bar 2.
3. Practice the transition between bars 1 and bar 2.
4. Practice bars 1 and 2 together.
5. Practice bar 3.
6. Practice the transition between bars 2 and 3,

7. Practice bars 2 and 3 together.

8. Etc

This way you can work through the song in focused slices. When you complete larger sections of the song (e.g. the phrase or verse), practice playing through those larger sections.

Eventually, you will be able to tie those sections together into the entire song.

Tips for Studying

Use Diagrams and Notation Examples

Words are terrible, music theory needs… music! When taking notes make sure you do so in a format that makes sense for the information that you are trying to remember. Do not go and write a paragraph of prose to describe a music theory concept - use notation or diagrams with supporting text to explain specific features of your diagram/notation.

Pace Yourself

Take your time, it's not a race. It is easy to fall into the trap of "I read X pages today therefore I am making progress". It doesn't matter how many pages you read if you don't understand them!

Take your time and make sure you understand the material that you are working on.

Have a Schedule

Regularly scheduled time is the best way to approach learning anything. If you read something once a week, by the time you come back to it next week you will have forgotten what you covered.

Every day is best and every couple of days is also effective. Having said that, once a week is better than nothing! Schedule your time on paper at the start of the week.

The Fastest Way to Learn

Without a doubt, the fastest way to learn is to find the best possible teacher, throw money at them and study with them part-time/full-time. After attending music college, studying books and courses, and studying with various teachers and courses; I can say without a doubt that the fastest I progressed was by taking 1-2-1 lessons with an excellent teacher. However, this is expensive and time-consuming and may not be an option for most people.

This was closely followed by a well-organised course of lessons I took. A good course is better than a mediocre teacher.

One thing to bear in mind is that you don't necessarily have to study with a teacher full-time. You could take lessons for a few months, or do intensive lessons for a week to get material to practice and study throughout the year.

Section 4: Your Equipment

There are a few things worth saying about equipment for your practice and creativity.

Guitar Tone

One of the easiest ways to make your music sound good is to have a good tone. If you read about tone online, you will find a lot of misinformation, so let's quickly clear up what we are referring to.

Guitar tone is the timbre of a particular note. It is the sonic quality of the note. If you take two different amplifiers (or even instruments) and play the same note the same way, it will sound different. This difference in sound is the timbre, and when we refer to tone, technically we are referring to timbre.

Note ornamentation is how a particular note is played. Is the player sliding into the note? Are then bending into the note? How fast is the bend? Are they using vibrato? What is the depth, width and timing of that vibrato?

When you read about tone being "in the fingers", that is a mistake. What the writer means is that ornamentation is in the fingers. It is a player's ornamentation that gives them their unique sound, it is due to ornamentation that Yngwie Malmsteen playing through a $30 amplifier still sounds like Yngwie Malmsteen.

What Affects Tone?

Several factors affect your tone, roughly in the following order:

1. Amplifier
2. Effects
3. Pickups
4. Strings
5. Guitar Body
    1. The tone control on the guitar

The Amplifier

Your amplifier will have the biggest effect on tone. There are several types of amplifiers that are available today:

- Valve
- Solid State
- Modelling

How Amplifiers Work

Before we look at what these different types of amplifiers are and how they work, we should probably talk a little about how amplifiers work in general.

When you play an electric guitar, the string vibrates. The string is vibrating above a pickup. The pickup is a set of magnets that are wrapped in electrical wire - there is a “wrapped magnet” underneath each string. When the guitar string vibrates inside this magnetic field an electrical voltage is “induced” in the wire around the pickup.

If you want to learn more about how this works, look up “Faradays Law of Induction” online.

This voltage then goes from the guitar, through the cable, into your amplifier. Your amplifier has several controls, but the basics of what it does is to use your guitar output to regulate a more powerful signal.

You can imagine the amplifier is a powerful river with a gate. The output from your guitar regulates how open or closed the gate in the river is, controlling how much of the powerful river can flow through the gate.

This variation in the flow of the powerful river matches the varying voltage coming from your guitar - it’s like taking a small key and cutting a much bigger key that has the same shape.

This is how you take the weak signal from your guitar and turn it into something powerful enough to be heard from your amplifier speaker.

Amplifiers are usually broken into three sections:

- Pre-amp
- Power amp
- Speaker cabinet

The pre-amp is a section that does most of the tone shaping. You can fiddle with EQ buttons and overdrive here. The power amp is mainly what we described above, it’s the bit that makes your guitar signal loud. The speaker cabinets are the speakers - they take the powerful signal from the power amplifier and turn it from electricity into sound.

All three of these sections affect your tone.

Combo amps are amps with all three sections built into one. “Heads” are a box that combines the pre-amp and power amp. “Cabs” are speaker cabinets that you can plug your head into.

Speaker cabinets can have different speakers in them, which has a big impact on tone. They can also come in different sizes, be “chambered” (this is the internal construction) and be built from different thickness woods, which can affect the tone.

Rack units are effectively a way to “build your own amp”, where the pre-amp and power amp are separate. This gives you more control over the tone. Racks are usually MIDI controlled, which is a system whereby you can press one button on a pedal board and change all your pre-amp and effects settings at once.

You may have seen inputs and outputs on your amplifier labelled “effects loop”. This gives you a way to put guitar effects between the pre-amp and power amp.

Solid State Amplifiers

“Solid State” refers to the method by which the signal is amplified. In a solid-state amplifier, transistors are used to control the amplification. There are different types of transistors which can affect the quality of the signal.

The big benefit to using transistors is that they are cheap and reliable - they last forever.

Valve Amplifiers

These, unsurprisingly, use valves to amplify the signal. Valves are also known as vacuum tubes. Vacuum tubes were used in the first electronic computers before moving into commercial technology. They were used in everything from old TV sets to AM/FM radio.

These days most valve electronics are obsolete, they're only being used in high-end hi-fis and guitar amplifiers.

Due to how valves work, when they are pushed hard, the signal that is being amplified starts to break down in a way that is deemed favourable, which is the source of valve overdrive. Valve amplifiers tend to sound best when they are pushed hard, to create more of this signal breakdown (hence the term "overdrive" from the valves being driven hard).

Generally speaking, valve amplifiers are accepted as having the best guitar tone.

The benefit of valve amplifiers is the sound.

The downside is that they are more expensive, heavier and require expensive maintenance - the valves will fail over time and need to be replaced.

Modelling Amplifiers

Modelling amplifiers seek to take the distortions that a valve introduces into the guitar signal, and model how that distortion behaves. The model is put into an algorithm and applied to your guitar signal.

This is what units such as the Kemper and Fractal Axe FX do.

The benefits of modelling units are that they are much more portable than a valve amplifier. They are also more reliable. Usually, they are plugged straight into a PA system or a speaker cabinet.

Cost-wise, they are usually about the same price or more than a full valve setup (head and cab).

The sound quality is very close, but usually not quite the same as a valve amplifier.

Effects

The next biggest impact on your tone will be from your effects. There are many types of effects that you can use and they will impact your tone.

There are two ways the effects can impact your tone:

- The way they change your sound (the effect they are adding).
- The quality of the DAC in the pedal (if it has it).

DAC stands for "Digital to Analogue Converter". This is sometimes known as A/D/A, "Analogue to Digital to Analogue". The signal coming out of your guitar is analogue - it's a continuously varying voltage. Some guitar pedals will use a tiny computer (a couple of microchips) inside the pedal to add the effect. This computer requires the signal from the guitar (analogue) to be chopped up and quantised via a DAC, after which it will process the signal (add the effect) and then take the digital signal and put it back into analogue.

If the DAC is cheap, it can hurt the tone. Most higher-end pedals will be fine for this (bear in mind that all music you listen to has been through multiple rounds of A/D/A conversion.

The negative influence that effects can have on your tone is known as "tone suck". A good way around this is to have a completely dry signal (dry means no effects, wet means effects have been added) with the effects added on top of the dry signal. This can be done in stereo and is known as a W/D/W setup (wet dry wet). Big rack systems sometimes use W/D/W to create a huge guitar sound.

Pickups

The next biggest factor in your tone is the pickups in your guitar. If your guitar has come with "stock" i.e. manufacturer-supplied pickups, you will find a big difference by changing them to top-tier pickups. As a note, higher-end guitars tend to come with good pickups.

There are two types of pickups:

- Active
- Passive

Passive pickups are magnets wrapped in wire and that's it. Active pickups use fewer turns of higher gauge wire than passive pickups - this results in lower output than passive pickups, so they have a small pre-amp built into them, which requires a battery to run and in turn leads to a higher output than passive pickups.[7]

Active pickups are often popular amongst extreme metal players. Passive pickups tend to have a more organic feel.

An additional consideration with your pickups is how close they are to the strings. When the pickups are raised, they will give a higher output, but the magnetic field of the pickup will fight against the vibration of the strings, reducing the length of time that the strings will ring out(known as the sustain).

When the pickups are lowered, they are further from the strings, reducing the output but increasing the sustain.

Balancing output and sustain takes a bit of trial and error - this is something that a luthier or tech may do for you when setting up your guitar.

Strings

Your strings will have an impact on your tone and playability. New strings have a clear tone and are usually a bit easier to play. Old strings can muddy your tone slightly, but a bit harder to play and also stick to your fingers a little.

There are several different companies making strings, some of which use different metals for the strings. You can find review videos online (something YouTube is great for). Strings also have different gauges, which is the thickness of the string. Again, there are some good YouTube videos comparing string gauges.

---

7 https://blog.andertons.co.uk/labs/active-vs-passive-pickups

How Often Should You Change Your Strings?

String manufacturers, for some reason, tend to recommend that you change your strings every 10 seconds. I usually follow these rules:

- Change your strings for gigs/recording sessions
- When practising, change them every month or so
  - Maybe less if you're trying to save a few quid

In general, when your higher strings start to discolour, they are starting to lose tone. When dirt is collecting on the back of the string, they are due for a change!

Guitar Body

The final factor in your tone is the guitar itself - the woods it is made out of and the way the neck is attached to the body. The are two possible ways to attach the neck to an electric guitar:

- Neck-Thru
- Bolt-on

Bolt-on is where the neck is bolted onto the guitar. The neck will sit in a socket on the guitar with a few large bolts in the back to hold it on.

Neck-thru construction is where the neck is an integral part of the guitar body. The neck will run through the length of the guitar body, with extra parts attached to the side to fill out the body.[8]

These effects on tone are minimal compared to other factors but can make a difference.

[8] https://en.wikipedia.org/wiki/Neck-through-body_construction

Guitar Tone Control

This is a dial, usually the lower dial, on your guitar. It has a small capacitor and it is used to remove some of the high-end from your output signal. Some guitar players like to remove this from their guitars.

Tone Blocks

At the body end of your guitar, the strings attach to the bridge. Increasing the mass of the bridge will cause the strings to vibrate for a longer time and can affect the frequencies in the string (i.e. frequencies that would normally be lost have a chance to exist for longer).

This can be accomplished by what is called a "tone block", which is a large block of metal screwed into the back of your bridge.

They can make a big difference - I was pleasantly surprised by how my guitar sounded after having one fitted.

Cables

Cables do not affect your tone. There is a lot of pseudoscience and voodoo around cables. The best thing for a cable is to get something that is tough so that it doesn't break easily, and is well shielded to prevent it from acting like an antenna and picking up other electromagnetic signals.

Guitar Tone for Practice

When practising and developing your technique, you don't want to have too much reverb/delay etc on your sound - this is because they can make it difficult to hear your timing too accurately. By all means, use a little, but use it very sparingly. When working on technique I like to use a clean, dry tone.

Improving Your Tone

To wrap up, if you want to improve your tone, work through the above list in the above order - change the biggest factors first, e.g. your amplifier, then work through the rest of the list in order.

Your Guitar

Higher-end guitars are usually nicer to play and are built with better-quality components. I have always loved Ibanez guitars and that's all I play. You can usually get a quite good deal on second-hand Ibanez's saving up to 50% on the new price.

When you buy a guitar, it's usually worth taking it to a luthier/guitar technician to get the guitar "setup". This involves changing the strings (something you can do easily yourself) but also setting the intonation and neck balance. Setting intonation and neck balance is something you can do yourself, but you have to know what you are doing - it's a complex job and easy to make mistakes.

The setup can also include pickup height adjustment and pole height adjustment.

Having your guitar set up properly makes a big difference to how playable it is, often feeling like a different instrument.

A good luthier will also be able to make little adjustments to the guitar to make it more playable and fix any slight manufacturing defects, which cheaper instruments tend to have. For example, the neck socket on my Ibanez was ever so slightly larger than the neck - my luthier inserted a piece of rubber into the joint to create a perfect fit.

If you are doing some serious recording or getting ready to play some gigs, getting your guitar set up will help give you an edge.

For those that are interested, I've had the pickups replaced, had the frets dressed (three times, eventually replacing the frets with stainless steel frets), replaced a broken volume control and fitted a tone block to the back of the bridge.

Fret Dressing

As you play the guitar, the metal strings are pressed against the frets. Over time, the frets will become worn down and flattened. This creates poor contact when the string is pressed against it, which can create buzz.

"Fret dressing" is when the fret is filed and reshaped to create perfect contact with the string. How many times your frets can undergo this process is dependent on the size of the fret, a bigger fret can be filed more times than a smaller fret.

Finding a Good Luthier / Technician

A luthier is someone who can build a guitar. A guitar technician (often shortened to "tech" or "guitar tech") adjusts guitars but does not build them. There is often some overlap between what they can do.

Finding a reliable and knowledgeable luthier/guitar tech can be a tricky thing to do, and like many things, often takes a bit of trial and error. The best way is via the personal recommendation of someone you know. If you take lessons, your teacher will probably know a reliable luthier that you can use.

I had to work my way through 3 guitar techs before finally finding someone who was competent at their job.

Home Studio

If you are creating your own songs, chances are you will be using some version of a home studio, whether it's simple or complex.

We'll look at the basics of a home studio, and a few upgrades you can consider getting and then we'll talk about all the components.

There are roughly four levels of home studio:

1. Your basic setup will be a computer, headphones an interface and a DAW.
2. Computer, interface, DAW and studio monitors.
3. Computer, interface, DAW, studio monitors, amp with power soak and impulse response modelling (software or hardware).
4. Computer, interface, DAW, studio monitors, amp, live room or isolation box with microphones for the amp speaker cabinet.
5. Purpose-built studio.

Level 1 is someone with their laptop, level 5 is a purpose-built studio.

Home Studio Components

Computer

This is the nexus of your studio. You'll need a computer with:

- USB ports for a sound interface and external storage.
- at least 8GB of RAM (ideally 16GB, or even 32GB)
- Intel i5 3GHz quadcore processor, Apple M1 processor, or better
- Enough storage for your compositions. A recorded song in a DAW can run to 300MB-700MB depending on how many tracks you are using (or more). 250GB internal drive with an external drive is a good starting point. If the internal and external drives are solid-state, even better.

I use a late 2015 (it's 2022 when I'm writing this book, so this computer is currently 7 years old) iMac, with a 3.2Ghz Quad Core Intel i5 with 8GB of RAM. My computer is fast enough for doing recording (one track at a time), working with a virtual orchestra and recording rock music with sample libraries.

It slows down a little and playback starts and stops with bigger projects, so I'll upgrade the RAM to 16GB or 32GB sometime soon, but for 90% of what I do with it, it's fine.

The point is, you need a computer that is good enough, but it doesn't have to be a supercomputer. But do make sure you check the specifications for any software/plugins/libraries/equipment you intend to use.

Sound Interface

This is a box that you can plug into your computer, and then plug instruments, microphones, headphones, studio monitors and other musical equipment into.

At a basic level, you can get a USB dongle with an input for your guitar and an output for your headphones. These can go for around £20, Behringer makes something like this that I started with.

The next level up is something that can handle studio monitors, headphones, two guitars or microphones; with gain controls and line/instrument inputs. The Focusrite Scarlett 2i4 is an excellent option at this level (I've used mine for years now and many students love them). These are great for recording vocals, guitar or other instruments where you need a maximum of two microphones. These cost around £130-£200. They can handle line, instrument or XLR inputs with a variety of outputs.

The difference in price for similar interfaces is usually down to features and the quality of the audio-to-digital conversion (known as DAC for "Digital analogue converter"). Higher-quality DACs are usually more expensive.

You only start to need more complex interfaces if you want to record multiple instruments or microphones at once. For example, if you are recording drums, you can need a minimum of 10 microphones. Usually, at this level, rack interfaces with plenty of inputs are used. You will also need a powerful computer to track that many microphones at once.

Headphones

You need some way to listen to what you have recorded. Good speakers are expensive, so if you are on a limited budget, I would recommend a semi-decent pair of studio headphones.

Your headphones should be wired. Wireless, or Bluetooth, headphones can have a small amount of latency. When you are just listening to music for fun, this isn't a problem, but when you are recording this latency will be noticeable and incredibly annoying.

When using the headphones, plug them directly into your sound interface.

Have them set loud enough, but don't go blasting your ears with them. Also be aware that with prolonged use, your ears get "used" to loudness, so for a given loudness, it can be perceived as getting quieter as time goes on, leading to increasing the volume over and over, which is a recipe for long-term hearing damage.

When using headphones, take them off every 20 minutes or so to give your ears a little rest and "reset" your perception of volume.

Monitors

Monitors is a fancy name for "good quality speakers". Normal PC speakers aren't good enough - they have a limited frequency response. Ideally, you want something that is powered, with separate bass and treble cones. You'll need speaker cables to connect the monitors to your sound interface (usually, these are not included with the monitors!).

I've found the M Audio BX-8 to be pretty good for this.

Set up your monitors so they form two points of an equilateral triangle, with you forming the third point. They should be pointing directly at you.

Good monitors can cost £300 for a pair.

Power Soak / Load Box

This is a device you can plug your power amp into that will make the signal smaller. Valve amplifiers sound best when they are turned up loud, but if you are recording at home, this may not be practical and you may well get complaints from your neighbours/housemates (not to mention damaging your hearing) unless you can put your amp in an isolated room.

Additionally, you cannot plug the output of your amplifier into your sound interface, as the signal will be too strong and will damage the sound interface.

A power soak is a device that is placed between the amplifier and speaker cabinet, which makes the signal quieter without, in theory, losing any of the tone.

Popular models include THD Hotplate, Marshall Powerbrake and Two Notes Torpedo range.

Many load boxes come with a line out which allows you to plug the output of the load box into your sound interface.

There are good YouTube videos demonstrating the difference between different load boxes.

Impulse Response

Everything in your signal chain affects your tone, including, as we mentioned earlier, your speaker cabinet. Impulse Response software/hardware will model the effect of a speaker cabinet on your tone.

This usually comes as software, but there are also hardware variants. A company called Two Notes has software and hardware solutions that you can look into.

Many modern DAWs come with plugins that will load impulse responses, and Two Notes offer a free plugin you can use with your DAW.

Isolation Box

This is a large wooden and padded box that you can place your speaker cabinet in, along with a microphone. It is acoustically insulated so that sound can't escape, meaning you can turn up your amp nice and loud without it disturbing anyone or blasting your ear drums.

These are a good solution to recording at home and if you don't want to buy one, you can build one.

These can sound a little "dead" compared to a nice studio room, but they are a great solution to recording your nice amp at home.

Microphones

If you are recording your guitar "micced up", you will need a microphone. When it comes to recording guitar cabinets, the industry standard is the Shure SM57.

Set the microphone up using a mic stand, pointing directly at one of your speaker cones, as close as you can get to the speaker cone.

The exact position of the microphone will affect the tone that you capture.

My album Impetuous Desire was recorded using a single SM57.

Some people like to use an additional microphone elsewhere in the room to capture the "ambience". When using multiple microphones you have to be careful that they are in phase. Going into the complexities of phase is outside the scope of this book, but a quick Google will tell you all about it.

Live Room

If you want to go all out you can go and build a live room. This is a sectioned-off room that has thick walls for sound isolation. It may or may not have a window. This will let you record amplifiers and other instruments easily and to a very high quality.

Some people build these in their basement or build a studio in their garden that has a live and control room.

When you go this far, you can create studio-quality recordings at home - while the best option, this is also the most expensive… and most fun!

Section 5: Your Environment

An often neglected area of practice is controlling your environment. People have argued for millennia over whether or not human beings have free will or if we are merely products of our environment.

The truth is we have free will, and our environment makes using that in certain ways easier or harder.

So by using our free will to influence our environment, we can make our practice much more effective. Let's dive into exactly how to do that.

Minimise Distractions and Enhance Your Focus

There are a handful of variables that will affect the rate at which your guitar playing will improve:

- Time spent practising
- What you are practising
- How you are practising
- How focused you are when you practice

By making sure we are highly focused, we will learn faster. If you spend less time practising but are highly focussed, you will learn faster than if you spend more time practising with low focus, with the ideal situation being more time practising in a highly focussed state.

So make sure you minimise distractions. The first thing to do is make sure that you are not doing anything else when you are practising - do not practice while watching TV, listening to music, watching YouTube etc.

Keeping your practice space tidy and neatly organised will also help you focus on the task at hand.

Guitar practice time is for guitar practice that's it.

Third-Party Distractions

You also want to minimise external distractions, distractions that are caused by others. Close those extra windows on your computer, put your phone on airplane mode, and turn off your email alerts.

If there are other people around you, ask them not to disturb you for the next XYZ minutes. When it comes to your significant other and children, you may have to make some adjustments, but try and find a system that works for everyone.

If you are constantly having your practice interrupted over things that can wait, you are going to struggle to focus and make progress.

A great benefit of a dedicated home studio is that you can shut the door and leave the outside world behind to focus on your music.

Have Your Environment Setup to Practice

This is easier to implement for some than it is for others, but the more dedicated your environment is to practice the better.

The best possible environment is a home studio/practice room whose only purpose is practising the guitar. But I realise that is not possible for everyone.

The next best thing is whatever your environment is, make it conducive to practice. You need to minimise the mental resistance to starting practice - often overcoming this resistance to getting started is harder than the practice itself.

This means that your guitar should always be out and ready to use. If you keep your guitar in a case, you have to get it out of its case before you practice. As silly as this sounds, it creates a bit of resistance that must be overcome before practice can start.

Here are a few things you can do to help decrease the resistance to getting started with practice:

- Guitar on a stand and ready to be used
- Guitar is plugged into an amplifier. All electrics are plugged into the wall and ready to be used.
- Practice material in order and on a music stand, near the guitar.
- The metronome and tuner are both on the desk and ready to be used.
- Picks within arms reach and ready to be used.
- Footrest under desk or nearby.
- Paper and pencil, if needed, ready and nearly organised.

As you can see, the main theme is that everything you could need to practice is out and ready, so that you just have to "step into" your practice space and you're ready to go.

I would also advise keeping your desk (if you are using one as part of your practice space) tidy and ready to be used. If you don't have a desk, I would strongly advise getting one! You can improvise a desk with a large flat piece of wood and two small chests of draws from Ikea, or find one second-hand. Either way, having a good-sized desk is great for productivity.

How to Practice With a Computer

There are some fantastic ways that we can use a computer and different programs to help us practice the guitar more effectively.

Often people use their computers incredibly ineffectively.

Let's get started with computers and tablets - they are not the same thing! A computer involves a screen, keyboard and mouse and a base station (a laptop will roll these into one - we'll count laptops and desktops as equivalent things). A tablet is a single screen.

Tablets are great at some things and not so great at others.

When it comes to guitar practice, I am yet to find an effective way to use a tablet. I have however found plenty of great ways to use a computer.

If you are going to set yourself up for practising and recording, then I would strongly advise using a computer and not a tablet. If money is tight, a second-hand iMac or mac mini is a good option.

Tablets are mainly for entertainment and browsing style activities, computers are for deep work.

There are one or two notable exceptions with using tablets for deep work, mainly for writing and composing music using notation; however, when it comes to practice, a computer is best.

There are two main areas to using a computer effectively:
- Using the correct programs.
- Using those programs effectively.

Using the Correct Programs

The types of programs that you use will fall into two main categories:

- Writing guitar tablature (usually called "tab" for short)

- Recording audio

Some programs will do both.

Why Write Guitar Tab?

If you are learning to play the guitar, you are going to be working through a lot of guitar tabs.

You will be getting exercises, maybe from a teacher, and writing out your ideas.

The benefit of using a computer program to write guitar tabs is that you can:

- Play the tab back so you can hear how it should sound.
- Add custom metronome/drum tracks to help you understand the rhythm (we go over how to do this in the appendix on programming metronomes).
- Store things efficiently so that you don't have 100s of pieces of paper lying around.
- Create backing tracks for pieces that you are practising.
- Slow down the song or exercise that you are learning.
- Compose ideas and share them with your friends to collaborate.
- Export your tab/scores to PDF/Audio/Print/MIDI/MusicXML etc.

Why Record Audio?

As a beginner, you will probably not need to record audio. In fact, given the learning curve that recording programs can have, I would recommend that you don't worry about this until you are reaching the late beginner / intermediate level (for most people this is after several months of lessons).

But when you do reach that level, it is a great tool.

Recording your playing will allow you to listen back to your playing and analyse your mistakes.

One thing that is quite useful is being able to visually see your recording against a grid, which visually tells you if your playing is in time or not, and if it isn't in time, you will be able to see if you're early, late, or just all over the place.

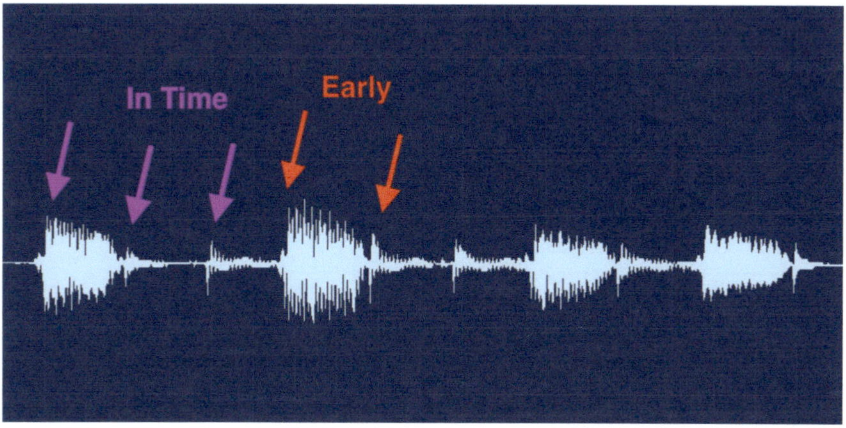

The grid lines are the faint white vertical lines. You can see where the recorded audio is in time (on the line) and out of time (in this case, before the line).

Recording programs become useful when you want to compose music. This could be anything from backing tracks to improvise over, to composing your own songs and instrumental pieces of music.

The top-level recording programs are known as Digital Audio Workstations, often abbreviated to DAWs.

DAWs will allow you to:

- Record and manipulate audio
- Input musical notes and play them back (via MIDI data)
- Use different sound libraries to play back your compositions (see below for an explanation)
- Control sound libraries from an external keyboard (for example, use your keyboard to play the cello!)
- Loop sections (very useful for practice)

- Mix / EQ and add effects to your tracks
- Use VSTs / AUs (see below for explanation)
- And more!

For example, you could record a guitar riff into a DAW, then loop it so that it plays several times in a row.

Every piece of professionally released music that you have listened to in the last 20 years has used a DAW.

DAWs are used for composing, recording, mixing and mastering music.

MIDI Data

MIDI stands for "Musical Instrument Digital Interface". This is a computer protocol for connecting musical instruments, usually keyboards, to computers and each other - a MIDI device can connect to a computer (via a sound interface) or other MIDI-capable devices.

MIDI is also a way to write musical notes to a computer file to share between different programs. Nearly all music programs can create MIDI files. For example, I can write a tab in Guitar Pro, export that to MIDI and open it in Logic Pro.

Sound Libraries

These are collections of pre-recorded sounds. Let's say you were writing a drum part for a guitar riff that you wrote. You could purchase a sound library where someone has recorded different parts of a drum kit, and these sounds are played back with your programmed drum part.

Sound libraries usually include different articulations, which are different ways of playing a note. A simple example is that a cello could be played arco (bowed) or pizzicato (plucked).

More articulations with better programming (how the library moves between notes) gives better quality and more realistic playback, but also tend to make libraries more expensive.

Sound libraries exist for every instrument imaginable, including orchestral instruments and the human voice. They are a great way to make realistic demos and are used in commercial releases.

For those that want a challenge, you can even record your own sound library.

There is an appendix at the end with some recommendations on different sound libraries you can try.

VSTs / AUs

VST stands for "Virtual Studio Technology" and AU stands for "Audio Unit". VSTs are used for Windows systems and AUs are used for Apple systems (Logic Pro and Garageband).

They accomplish the same thing - they allow you to add extra software to your DAW so that it can do more stuff. This could be anything from a reverb plugin, to a software guitar amplifier, to a sound library that allows you to play back any orchestral instrument realistically.

Software companies typically release their products in both VST and AU versions.

Program Recommendations

For writing tab, I recommend:

- Guitar Pro - Creates professional-looking guitar tabs and plays them back. Guitar Pro is designed around a "tab first" input. You can add chord and scale diagrams to your tabs, and compose for multiple instruments. It's designed for guitar players. It's great for writing songs, exercises and collaborating with other musicians. Guitar Pro retails at around $80.

- MuseScore - This is a program designed around musical notation input. If you are wanting to compose for classical instrumental, or compose "notation first" rather than "guitar first", MuseScore is great. It can also do guitar tabs but does not give you as many articulation options as Guitar Pro does for guitar. MuseScore is free. MuseScore is a bit harder to use than Guitar Pro.

For a DAW, I recommend:

- Logic Pro (or other DAW). Great for recording and editing audio, and composing. I now use Logic Pro for writing tabs. Logic Pro costs around $200. One feature I love is Logic can scroll through a tab while you record it.

Other DAWs that are popular:

- Pro Tools. Has more audio editing options than Logic Pro (but you probably don't need these), but isn't as good at handling MIDI as Logic Pro. Pro Tools will only work with specific hardware.
- Cubase. Recording and MIDI editing. My metal album, Impetuous Desire, was recorded in Cubase. Hans Zimmer (film score composer) uses Cubase for composing movie scores.
- Studio One. A couple of my students use this. I haven't used it myself. It's cheap and they seem happy with it.
- Reaper. This is "Shareware", so you can use it for free or pay the $25 for a licence. Reaper allows you to record and edit audio, use VSTs etc. It seems similar in capability to Cubase, but without the price tag. It has a big community and is becoming very popular.

Using Computer Programs Correctly

Music technology programs are complex programs. They can do an enormous amount to make your life easier... if you learn how to use them.

Many students settle for a very basic understanding of the programs they use, and this hinders them by slowing down their workflow.

For example, let's say you wanted to enter a riff that repeats 20 times. You could type out that riff 20 times. Or you could type it out once and then copy and paste it 20 times.

This is a simple example, but the point I'm making is this - these programs are packed with features that will make your life easier… if you learn how to use them.

Read the manual for these programs.

Watch YouTube tutorials.

Reach out and ask questions - all of these programs have forums, Facebook groups, and subreddits with communities that will help answer your questions.

If you ever find yourself using a program and thinking "It would be nice if…" then the feature you are after probably exists. Read the manual, ask a question and see if someone knows the answer. If the feature doesn't exist, another user may be able to recommend a different way of approaching the problem.

Keyboard Shortcuts

Another vital part of using computer programs correctly is learning keyboard shortcuts. Using the mouse to do everything in these programs is horribly inefficient.

We spent a large section of this book dealing with how to make your guitar practice more efficient, you want to apply this search for efficiency to the programs that you use.

As an example of using programs efficiently, I often practice using Logic Pro. I will set up a backing track for the piece I am practising, and focus on a particular section.

Now, I could use my mouse, press play, play the section, get my mouse again, press stop, move the play head back to the start, press play again… or, I can set up a loop, and press the spacebar to start and let the loop play over and over for me to practice to. Then press the space bar to stop.

Which method would you rather use? For a given amount of practice time, my method with the loop will allow you to get more repetitions in. It will also be less stressful because all you have to think about is your guitar playing, you don't have to fiddle around with the mouse and set up the program for every repetition.

Programs like Logic Pro are highly customisable with keyboard shortcuts, allowing you to assign a shortcut to nearly every function.

Over large periods these workflow and time-saving "hacks" compound to make incredible differences in the total time you spend actually on your guitar.

Yes, it is something else that you have to go and learn. Yes, these programs have a steep learning curve.

But work through it, and long term you will reap the rewards in your playing.

Using Templates

Templates are a fantastic way to save a lot of time and work. When setting up Guitar Pro or your DAW, you may find that you are doing a lot of the same things. Maybe you are always adding the same instruments. Maybe you are always loading the same virtual instruments and adding the same AU/VSTs over and over again. Maybe you are making the same changes to your score settings.

You can get your computer to do all of this for you.

Open a blank file/project and add all the things that you would typically add. Change the layout and score settings to things you normally use. Then save that file as a template.

Next time you want to use those settings in a project, all you have to do is load that template and everything is loaded for you - huge time savings!

You may want to make a few templates for the different types of projects you use. For example, in Logic Pro, I have a template for rock songs and a template for orchestral projects.

Labelling Your Tabs / Scores

When creating a tab/score, it should be correctly labelled. When composing you will know exactly what you are doing, but if you were to revisit your score in a few months, you will probably find that you have forgotten a lot of what you have done and why.

You should label:

- Title
- Structure
- Harmony (chord names and numerals).
- The composer

Organise Your Files

Once you have been playing the guitar for a while, you will start to accumulate a lot of computer files. Tabs, songs, backing tracks and exercises; it is easy to end up with 100s of files.

You want to make sure they are organised so that you can find them. This means using suitable file names. “New Song” is not helpful. “Exercise 2” is not helpful. Use a file name that describes the file.

Using a sensible file name will also make it easy to search your files for what you are looking for.

Create a directory structure that makes sense. For example, you could organise your exercises into:

- Scales
- Sweep picking
- Chords
- Theory
- Rhythm

I took lessons from a great guitar player called George Bellas for a few years. I would copy his lessons twice, once into a date-based hierarchy, which made it easy to track exercises and assignments for submission week by week, and then I would copy every lesson into a category-based hierarchy, which has made it easy for me to reference lessons years later.

CMD + S Twitch and Backups

Save, save, save. When working, you want to constantly be saving your work as you go. Learn the keyboard shortcut (remember that whole section on learning keyboard shortcuts properly...?) so that you can save in a split second while you are working, without interrupting your workflow.

Make sure you have backups. If you use a Mac, the built-in program Time Machine is a fantastic way to create backups automatically as you go. You'll want an external hard drive that you can leave plugged in for backups.

There is a program called Backblaze which offers very cheap, secure and automated cloud backups of your files.

Computer Specifications

How powerful a computer do you need? I've been using a late 2015 iMac since... well around 2015 (I'm writing this in 2022). It has a 3.2GHz Intel Quad Core i5 and 8GB RAM. When running my DAW (Logic Pro) I'll make sure everything else is closed and it can handle everything I throw at it ok.

Apple is my preference but it's not necessary. I tend to find Apple computers age well compared to Windows machines.

I've run a full orchestra through sample libraries and recorded rock music and it has been able to manage, now and then having to pause and start again because the RAM is maxed out.

So 8GB is manageable, but you may want 16GB or even 32GB if your budget can handle it.

Any modern computer with 8GB RAM should be fine for recording a rock band track by track with some virtual instruments. If you are going to record multiple instruments at once, have dozens of tracks playing back at once and many virtual instruments, get as much RAM as possible.

Section 6: Healthy Living

This is a book on learning guitar and creativity, why are we talking about health?

Firstly, I am not a doctor and this is not medical advice. If you want to improve your health, talk to your doctor. These are just ideas that I have found useful. You should use this section as a list of things to research and a recollection of my own experiences.

There is a modern trend of treating the mind and body as separate entities. In philosophy, this is a problem referred to as "The mind-body dichotomy". The mind and the body are two parts of the same thing - a human being.

A healthy mind helps have a healthy body, and vice versa. Taking care of your health helps your mind work more effectively, which in turn helps you be more creative.

Here are a few things that I have found useful:

What You Put Into Your Body

Food is a modern vice. 63% of adults in the UK are overweight[9]. Over 73% of adults in America are overweight[10]. While it is a testament to the modern world that we can supply calories in abundance at a lower cost than ever before in human history, it has become a problem.

---

9 https://www.cancerresearchuk.org/health-professional/cancer-statistics/risk/overweight-and-obesity

10 https://www.medpagetoday.com/primarycare/obesity/90142

Controlling the food you eat is an important part of looking after your health.

You want to keep an eye on how much of the following you consume:

- Processed food
- Refined sugar
- Seed oils / refined oils
- Flour

If you are eating trash, try to find healthier substitutes, you probably eat a lot of what you do from habit, not from enjoyment.

Make sure that you get enough protein.

If you have things like fizzy drinks, replace them with water with some apple or lemon - fizzy drinks are a disaster for your health. Foods with vegetable oils/seed oils are also quite bad for your health. There is a great book called "The Mood Cure" which goes over the effects these substances have on your body.

This doesn't mean don't have fun food - but save them as a weekly treat rather than something you eat every day. Having something each day that is around 10% of your daily calories is a good way to have something "fun".

It goes without saying that if you are abusing drugs or having an excess of alcohol, removing those from your "Diet" will be incredibly beneficial!

Try and focus on fresh whole foods, such as fresh meat and fresh vegetables. Cook using roasting or butter and avoid using seed oils / processed oils.

Exercise

Have a walk every day, ideally two walks. Do some resistance training a few times a week. One of the most time-effective workouts I've tried is "Convict Conditioning" by "Coach Paul Wade". This book is a series of bodyweight exercises you can do 2-3 times a week. They don't take very long, sometimes 20 minutes for a workout.

Simple and Sinister by Pavel Psatsouline is a great guide to using a kettlebell for a daily workout (disclaimer, I haven't used this program but it's on my list to try).

I don't recommend other exercise regimens such as CrossFit. I did CrossFit for a couple of years, and while I got quite strong quite quickly, I also took more injuries than I'd have liked. Bodybuilding is effective for increasing strength but can wear out your joints over time, and people who do bodybuilding to an extreme degree tend to die young.

Fasting

Something I've particularly enjoyed is fasting. There is an idea in the modern world that we need to eat "3 square meals a day", and with snacks in between, we're effectively eating nearly every waking hour.

Intermittent fasting is a great way to help lose some weight and also free up some time. I usually eat between 2pm and 8pm. I rarely feel hungry in the mornings and use the time I save to do something useful - like work on my guitar playing!

I know that some people love breakfast foods (in my opinion, they're the best foods), so I still enjoy them. I sometimes have a cooked breakfast as my lunch.

My main meal is usually at 2pm, with meat, eggs, green vegetables, sometimes kale, and a natural carbohydrate (either rice or baked potatoes). My second meal at around 6-8pm is usually some wholewheat pasta with cheese on top.

There are several ways you can try intermittent fasting. One of my friends dropped a ton of weight recently when she stopped eating after 6pm. In general, the idea is that you eat inside an 8-hour window, and don't eat for 16 hours each day.

Longer fasts for 24 hours with just water (and some salt if you're feeling sleepy) are a good way to curb your appetite and rest your body - I usually do a 24-hour fast once or twice a week. I recently did a two-day fast and will be doing 3 and 4-day fasts in a couple of months.

Get Sunlight

If you are in California, southern Europe or somewhere similarly sunny, this won't apply to you so much, but if you are in a cloudy place such as northern Europe, then get more sunlight. Sunlight creates vitamin D which is vital for the immune system and general well-being/happiness. It also helps your body clock with your circadian rhythm.

Most people would benefit from spending more time outside in general and getting fresh air.

Something I've adopted into my mornings is to take 20-30 minutes to sit in my garden and listen to music. It's quite relaxing and it's enjoyable to listen to music rather than having it as a background to my day.

Section 7: Completing Projects

This entire section is something that I only came to understand relatively recently. In retrospect, like many things in retrospect, it seems obvious.

Be Prolific

A lot of the greatest creatives in history were prolific. A lot of people will think "I need to be creative to be prolific", but this logic is back to front, being prolific helps you become more creative.

There is a story of a pottery teacher who experimented with their class. The class was split in two. One half had to create one pot, they could take as long as they wanted to make it and their grade would be based on that single pot.

The other half of the class would be graded on the number of pots that they created.

Who made the best pots? You may be surprised that the half of the class that were prolific and created as many pots as possible ended up creating the best pots. Every time they made a pot they learned a little bit more about what does and doesn't work.

Reading and studying theory and composition is a vital part of becoming more creative, but it is a step in the right direction, eventually, you have to put pen to page and compose something.

And the more you compose, the more you will learn about what works and doesn't work, the more you will learn about weaknesses in your understanding that need correcting and the more you will learn about what you enjoy composing.

Perfectionism - What if it Sucks?

A stumbling block that creatives (and aspiring creatives) often face when it comes to being prolific is perfectionism. Believe me, I understand this.

In 2017 I released a heavy metal album called "Impetuous Desire". It's fair to say that it's pretty good. For three months before releasing it, I listened to it every night picking apart every tiny flaw I could find, wondering if I should just delete it.

In retrospect, that was a bit neurotic, but whatever you want to call it, perfectionism, Imposter Syndrome (Who am I to release music?) is a real psychological effect that you will have to face.

I've seen students go through this when they start composing music or recording their own songs, there is a real fear when it comes to releasing their creations to the public.

One of the most effective ways of I have found of dealing with this, is to take the following stance:

"It is not my job to judge my work. It is my job to create to the best of my ability, with as much effort as I can, and then to release it. It is someone else's job to judge it.".

How to Choose Your Next Project

Earlier we discussed the mindset of improving our playing, where we set perfection as the direction that we want to move in, and being 1% better than we were last week is the goal of practising.

We will use a similar idea for choosing the projects that we want to work on.

Dream Big, Move Small

Entertain big dreams. What does a big dream look like for you? Playing a show to 10,000 people? Releasing an album? Recording a song with an orchestra?

Take some time, right now to think about it for a moment. You'll know you've hit the right "big idea" when you get a jolt of excitement, maybe you'll have an uncontrollable smile when you picture yourself doing the "big idea".

Now break that big idea down into smaller ideas.

For example, let's say you want to, one day, compose an album. We could break down composing an album into the following steps:

- Compose an album
- Compose a song
- Compose a verse/chorus
- Compose a riff

So if you want to one day compose your own album, you can start today by writing a riff. Maybe you spend a few months or a couple of years composing riffs and learning how to arrange other instruments (drums, bass etc) around those riffs. Write 100 riffs. Then you have a go at writing a verse. Then write 50 verses.

Then you have a go at writing a full song. We are slowly moving up in levels of complexity.

Let's say you want to play a show for 10,000 people. We could break that down like this:

- Perform to 10,000 people (festival show)
- Perform to 1,000 people (small festival show)
- Perform to 500 people (club show)
- Perform to 100 people (bar show)
- Perform to 20 people (open mic night)

And now you have to figure out how to slowly move through this "ladder". For an open mic night, you need to learn a few songs. Maybe you can do instrumental songs, or you go down to watch a few times, find a singer, and ask if you can accompany them in a couple of weeks.

Once you've done a few of those, maybe you are going to look for a band you can join (or start) and play a few bar shows together. Most big cities will have 100s of places you can play at.

Once your band is getting regular experience playing and building a bit of a following, you can think about contacting promoters to position yourself to be an opening act for bigger bands coming through on tour.

Etc.

We start at a small level and slowly build up our ability. This process will take several years, but like anything else, if you just keep chipping away at it, you will make progress.

What's Possible at This Point in Time?

In the real world, we have limits on our resources. When deciding what projects we are going to take on, we have to know what is required to complete those projects and if we have the resources to do so.

If there is a mismatch between what the project requires and the resources we have, we need to find a way to "bridge the gap", so that our project becomes possible.

And usually, given the amount of technology that is available, there is a way to bridge the gap.

For example, let's say that you want to record an album, but you can't afford to hire a drummer and the studio time that a drummer would need. An album of drums would take 2-5 days depending on the drummer. At $250/day for a studio, we are talking $500-$1,250 in studio time. The drummer may want $50/hour. With 6-hour days, that's $300/day, so $600-$1,500 for your drummer, bringing you to a total cost of $1,100-$2,750 just to record drums!

Maybe that's in your budget, or maybe it isn't. What other options do you have?

You could find an online marketplace for session musicians (there are a few of these) and hire someone there who has a home studio and will record for $100/song. You now have studio-quality drums for $1,000 (assuming 10 songs on your album).

Is that too much?

You could use a drum sample library. A sample library is when someone records an instrument being played, such as a drum kit, and then plays those sounds back. So you program the sample library to play the snare at certain points, the hi-hats at others, etc.

Your sample library (for a drum kit) could be anything from $150 to $450. I'll include a list of sample libraries in the appendix.

Something worth pointing out is that you may have to apply just as much creativity to finding a way to see your project through to completion as you do in the project itself.

It's worth noting that finding a cheaper way to do something does not necessarily mean getting a worse result.

Here is a list of options that you can use for different projects, to help get your creative juices flowing:

Record drums for an album:

- Hire a famous drummer and go to a recording studio.
- Hire a drum teacher from a local music school and go to a recording studio.
- Hire a drum teacher from a music school that can record from home (I did this for the drums on Impetuous Desire and they sound great).
- Hire a session drummer online who can record.
- Hire a session drummer to record an electric drum kit and send you the MIDI data to put into a drum sample library.
- Program a drum sample library yourself.

Record guitars for your song:

- Goto a fancy studio with nice amps and record using their amps.
- Build a recording room to keep your amps in and record them.
- Record your own amps at home with a cabinet isolation box.
- Record your own amps at home with a microphone and a power attenuator.
- Use a Kemper / Axe FX / Amp Cloner. Get some good presets online.
- Use digital amp simulators such as Positive Grid BIAS.
- Use default digital amp simulators in Logic Pro X.

No matter what your level of resources is, there is something that you can do to get your project completed. Figure it out and do it. Sure, it might not be the quality that you want, but a completed project that is imperfect is better than a perfect project that never happens.

And you will probably find that as you complete projects, your ability to find ways to complete them and access to resources increases.

Choosing a Musical Direction

Some people know exactly what they want to do musically, and some don't. You will probably find that as you put more time into studying music, you become aware of options that you didn't know originally existed and what you are interested in develops.

You may find your original interests and musical desires change over time, and this is ok.

Some people aren't sure what they are interested in, so how can you become prolific if you are not sure what it is you want to do?

The best way to approach this is similar to how you would approach that problem with other areas in your life. Try out a whole bunch of different things, give them a serious go, and then spend some time reflecting on whether you enjoyed them or not. If you enjoyed them, then try more things in that direction. If you didn't enjoy them, ask yourself why - did you not enjoy it because:

- You tried something that was too far beyond your ability level? So maybe you would enjoy it in the future when you're at a higher level.
- You dislike everything about what you tried?

Or maybe there was only an element of the thing you tried that you disliked? Figure out what that "thing" is and try again.

Let's use some examples.

Let's say you aren't too sure about a genre that you like, so you choose 5 songs from different genres and over the next 5 months you are going to learn them. One of the songs you choose is a heavy metal song. When you listen to the song, it's quite exciting, but you struggle to play it, you just can't crack getting those riffs to sound correct and as a consequence, you don't enjoy the process of trying to learn this song.

Does that mean that you shouldn't try learning any metal songs? A better approach would be to try again with some easier songs in that genre or possibly choose sections of songs to play, rather than playing entire songs.

Maybe across the five genres you find that you can play the songs ok, but the whole process of learning other people's music is just boring to you. You enjoy playing the guitar and want to do more with it. In that case, maybe you need to explore improvisation and composition.

Maybe learning the songs isn't that interesting, but performing them gives you a thrill like nothing you've experienced in life?

Maybe learning the songs is ok and there are elements of each song you like, which you use as criteria to develop your taste in music and find other pieces to play?

By honing in on precisely what it is that we do and don't like, and can then create a hypothesis and experiments to find something that we do like, and then we can do more of that.

This process may take some time, and you may also find that figuring out precisely what it is you do and don't like is a challenge and takes a bit more introspection than you at first thought, but if you work the process you will find that you can deepen your enjoyment of music and the guitar.

Completing Projects

Most guitar players find it easy to start projects, and much harder to complete projects. Usually, guitar players who have been playing for a while have an archive of riffs, licks and ideas that they have created over the years… that sit on their computer gathering metaphorical dust.

It's important to be able to complete projects - not just start them!

There are a few possible components to this problem:

- Time management
- Knowledge gaps
- Insecurity
- Technology
- Premature judgement

You may find you have a mix of all four. Let's break down each one and see how it can impact completing projects and what you can do about it:

Time Management

Having a flash of inspiration, writing a cool riff and recording it and tabbing it out doesn't take very long. It may even take as little as 5-10 minutes.

However, writing out parts for other instruments, getting a structure together, and practising so you can play the parts accurately can take an enormous amount of time.

If you are struggling to complete projects, you may have to reorganise your priorities. For example, let's say that you currently practice for one hour a day. You do a 10-minute warm-up, 15 minutes on a scale, 15 minutes on improvisation, 10 minutes on theory and 10 minutes on writing new ideas. So you effectively have 10 minutes (your new ideas time) to work on completing your song.

It's probably going nowhere fast.

You may find that you have to reduce your other elements of practice to 5 minutes each so that you can spend 40 minutes a day completing your song.

Or, you use an A/B schedule (we covered this in the section on How to Practice), and do your guitar practice on Day A and work on your song on Day B.

Or maybe you change something else in your life so that you can put an extra hour a day into working on your song and getting your practice done.

Most problems on guitar can be solved with time, and completing a song is certainly one of them.

Knowledge Gaps - Collaboration

You may understand (or get the inspiration) to write a riff, but you may not understand how to write parts for drums, bass, voice or lead.

Or maybe you don't understand structure or form in music?

If you can identify these problems, you can then find resources or teachers to help you fix those problems. This can be a slow process, you may find that it takes a year or two to fix those knowledge gaps, but you will be a much more competent musician (and more creative!) after doing so.

You can also hire people to help you.

When I did Impetuous Desire, I had no idea how to write drum parts (something I have since rectified). I recorded demos of the guitar parts (recorded to a click) and sent them to a great drummer who made drum parts and recorded them (I think he did the entire thing in one to two days).

I was also quite poor at writing vocal melodies. I had the singer on the album improvise different vocal melodies and send me recordings. He would send me three takes of each instrumental demo with him going "oooh, aaaah, etc" over the top. I would then cut and edit the bits I liked best into one "master" demo, and then I wrote lyrics to that melody.

I found that the quality of my lyrics improved dramatically by having a good vocal melody to write to.

An interesting side note on the vocal melodies, there were some parts where I liked the melodies the singer had made, but the lyrics weren't right for that part of the song - I turned those sections into an instrumental break with some lead-guitar based on the vocal melody the singer had created.

When it comes to "structuring" how you collaborate, there are two ways:

- The collaborator takes a percentage of the songwriting credits.
- The collaborator is paid and you own 100% of the song.

How you structure things is up to you, but at a lower level, people will only collaborate to get paid (unless you are starting a band with someone).

Insecurity

Maybe you make a riff and then think to yourself "This sucks". The truth is, it's probably not as bad as you think. And even if it is, there are still plenty of people that enjoy awful music. As cheesy as it sounds, we are often our own worst critics. At the start of this section, we discussed perfectionism and that is quite applicable here.

Let's go with the idea that your riff does suck. So what? That doesn't mean that you suck, it just means that the little piece of music you wrote sucks. You don't have to show this to anyone or release it. Take the idea and roll with it, take your sucky riff and turn it into a whole song.

I guarantee that you will learn much more by taking a bad riff and turning it into a song, than by waiting to write the perfect riff before you start working on your songwriting.

The best way to write a great song is to write 100 bad songs.

No one has to hear them. Write 100 bad songs, accept that they won't be great but that you're working through a process (maybe they're practice songs?) and I guarantee that if you do go and work through writing 100 songs, you will write a few that you quite enjoy and can take some pride in.

Technology

Is there a problem with technology that is holding you back from completing your project? This was something that we discussed under "What's Possible at This Point in Time?". Can you borrow gear from a friend? Goto a practice studio and use gear there? Rent gear? Save up over time for a piece of gear? Make do with something that isn't quite as good?

If the problem is operating your gear/software, read the manual, ask a friend to help you, get help from a Facebook group/forum, find someone who knows how to use it and get lessons, or find a book on Amazon.

There are plenty of options. Figure something out and move forwards. Even if you aren't sure if you have a solution, give something a go, then evaluate and try again.

Premature Judgement

Sometimes we don't complete projects because we write off our ideas before they have had a chance to blossom.

As guitar players, we often have a "guitar-centric" view of writing music - we write some guitar parts and then arrange the other instruments around that. There is nothing wrong with this approach (we'll look at it, and others, later when we look at creativity techniques), but it is important to remember that there are other instruments.

Unless you are writing a piece where the guitar is the only instrument, you have to bear in mind that the guitar does not exist in a vacuum.

Even the simplest riff, for example, a few power chords, can sound incredible when matched with drums and bass guitar. There are plenty of great songs that do this.

So next time you have an idea, don't write it off. Have your idea, work on your idea, maybe refine it, create some variations... add some context to your idea with other instruments, and then decide if you want to keep it or not.

Only judge your idea once it is complete. I would go as far as not judging your ideas at all. Occasionally I will trash an idea if it isn't working, but most of the time I'll keep working on my ideas until they're finished as a complete song.

Dealing with Ideas

Once you start having ideas, what should you do with them? I would recommend that you record the idea somehow, whether that is a tab or a recording. I try to put all my new ideas into a new Logic Pro project, then I can record them and have the tab all within the same program - I can then easily work on it at a later date.

Try and give your idea a filename that is more descriptive than "New Idea 20", so you have some chance of remembering what it is when you next look at it.

And at a minimum, keep your new ideas inside the same folder on your computer.

What Do People Listen to When They Listen to Music?

Before we think about recording our music, it's worth thinking about what the average person is listening to when they listen to music.

There are two main things the average person is listening to when they listen to music:

- Production quality

    - This is the guitar tone, quality of the mix etc.
- Timing
    - Do the instruments sound in time?

Some genres defy these conventions, for example, punk and black metal. But even there, if you compare the successful commercial releases to the unsuccessful or more underground releases, you can see that these two factors are at play.

So when it comes to recording our musical creations, we want to make sure that we can play in time (which should be a given if you've been practising correctly) and we also want to make sure the production quality is as good as possible, from getting a great tone to mixing and EQing.

Recording Tips

Completing projects means that you're going to be doing a lot of recording, whether it's creating demos, going to a studio or recording at home. In this section, we'll cover a few tips on how to record effectively.

There are a few tools you should understand how to use within your DAW, which we'll outline here. Use this section as a list of things to check out and find some tutorials for. If there is demand for it, I'll create some tutorials on how to do the following inside Logic Pro.

You will be able to find tutorials on YouTube for how to do the following inside the DAW that you use. Note: Some entry-level DAWs won't have all these features, but all top-level DAWs will have them or something very similar.

Buy a Bass Guitar

Real bass is a great way to add some realism to your demos. Buy a cheap guitar and use a software amplifier inside your DAW and record bass parts onto your songs. It will feel a bit awkward at first, but it can be treated like an oversized guitar.

A bass guitar is great for songwriting and making demos.

Cross Fades

You will probably find that you record the song in sections, rather than recording it all at once.

When moving from one section of the song to another, you want to record an overlapping section. Say for example you are recording a verse that goes straight into the chorus. You record the verse and then record the chorus.

When recording the chorus, start from the last few chords of the verse. Then, create a "crossfade" between the two sections. A crossfade will fade out the first section while simultaneously fading in the new section.

This gives you a seamless transition across multiple recordings through the song.

Comping

Most modern DAWs will have what is called "comping". Learning how to use this will save you an enormous amount of time and very quickly speed up the quality of your recordings.

Comping is recording on a loop. You record multiple takes of the same section, then choose the bits you want from each take. When selecting the sections you want, the DAW will automatically "crossfade" between takes, to create a seamless take.

In and Out Fades

If you create a series of individual recordings within your DAW, you will notice that when you playback, you get a small series of "clicks" at the start and end of each sound file.

You can overcome this by creating small fade-ins and fade-outs on each file. You can do this with automation (not recommended), but many DAWs have the option for adding short fades on the inspector for the audio file - this is the best way to add these types of fades.

Order to Record In

When recording instruments, you usually want to record in the following order:

1. Drums
2. Bass
3. Rhythm Guitars / Clean Guitars
4. Vocals / Lead Guitars

Microphone Considerations

Part of the tone you get when recording guitars will come from the microphone, and the placement of the microphone. Usually, an SM57 is the microphone of choice for recording guitars. You may also want to use another microphone to capture the sound of the room - this can add a nice ambience to your recording. This ambience can also be added via a room modelling or reverb plugin.

For reference, Impetuous Desire was recorded using a single SM57 up close to the speaker (Celestion Vintage30 speakers).

If you are going to a studio, they should have a selection of microphones and also understand how to use them - this is part of what you pay for when going to a studio.

When using multiple microphones, you have to be aware of phase (again, in a studio this is something that the engineer should be taking care of). Phase can be thought of as how in time the microphones are with each other. A quick google of “microphone phase” will tell you all you need to know about this.

Tune the Guitar for the Range You're Using

The guitar is never exactly in tune. Due to some physics and convenience reasons, the frets on a guitar are all in slightly the wrong place. This is mostly compensated for by making sure the intonation is properly set (something a guitar tech will do for you when getting your guitar setup), but the frets are still slightly out.

If you are playing a particular range on your guitar for a recording, you may find you get a sweeter sound by tuning your guitar to that range. You will need a chromatic tuner for this.

For example, say you are playing a riff that is entirely around fret 7. Tune your strings to the note on fret 7, rather than the open string. You will find that the guitar sounds a bit nicer.

Additionally, when tuning strings, make sure you pick them as hard as you will be playing them. Sometimes when tuning, guitarists will "tickle" the string, then when it comes to playing will go absolutely to town on them.

Then tuning of the string changes ever so slightly the harder it is picked, so make sure you represent playing conditions when tuning.

Doubling Rhythm Parts

For almost every rock and metal song that you have ever listened to, the rhythm guitar has been doubled. This means it was recorded twice. One recording is panned slightly left and the other recording is panned to the right.

This creates a "wider" and thicker sound.

When doing this, you need to make sure that both rhythm parts are precisely in time. An easy way to check the timing is to listen back to the recording using headphones. Pan one recording to the left and one to the right. If the rhythm part is in time, you will hear the recording in the centre of the stereo field. If the recording is out of time, you will hear it "bounce" back and forth, left to right.

Give Yourself Extra Time

Things such as recording almost always take more time than you think they will. If you are going to a studio you will want to budget for this. Some studios may be open to an arrangement where you book 5 days and have the option to do 2 additional days at the end, or something to that effect - don't ask, don't get!

However much time you give yourself, put a few extra days on the end, you'll probably need it.

If going to a studio, you can also ask the engineer for their opinion on how much time you should need.

Why Use A Studio?

There are three main benefits to using a recording studio:

- The engineer
- The gear
- The focus

You get an engineer to operate the computer and set up the recording equipment. They'll help you get a good tone from your amp and problem solve any problems that will come up. They can also give you a second opinion on any decisions that have to be made while recording.

An experienced engineer will have a lot of... well experience, so while you don't have to do what they say, they can have valuable input. I always try to say something along the lines of I'll welcome their ideas but may decide differently.

All this allows you to focus on the guitar playing and let someone else deal with everything else.

Studios also have a ton of gear. Nice amps are expensive and a studio will usually have a few amps that you can choose from. This can help you get the best sound possible for your recording.

If you want session players, a studio will probably know people that can help you out - I found the main vocalist for Impetuous Desire through the recording studio I used to record the album.

If you want a commercial-quality recording, then go to a commercial studio - look at some albums you like, they usually list the recording studio in the liner notes. Look the studio up and ask for a quote.

The obvious downside to using a studio is the cost. Studios can range from £150/day to £350+ per day. However, that's the price of getting a professional sound.

The last main benefit is the psychological benefit. Often, our emotional states are partially tied to the location we are in. Going to a studio gives you a focused, distraction-free environment where you can fully apply yourself to the task at hand, and also have an "emotionally blank slate".

Something as simple as having someone else operate the DAW frees up your mind to focus on your playing. Having someone there to give you instant feedback is also very helpful.

Personally, working with great professionals in a studio is something I love doing. I'd recommend you try it at least once!

Two Methods of Recording

There are two ways you can record a band: Live or individually.

With live recording, the whole band is recorded live - sometimes without the singer. Each instrument is micc'ed up and there are often sound isolation panels between amplifiers and the drummer. Solos are often added afterwards.

The benefit of recording this way is that you will get a more natural sound. Often the vocalist will record their parts separately - apart from anything else this helps save their voice. A singer can't sing for the same amount of time that a guitarist can play, usually, singers are limited to being able to sing for a couple of hours a day before their voice gets tired.

By recording separately, the singer doesn't have to do the same parts over and over again when someone else in the band makes a mistake.

A downside to recording this way is that there will be "bleed" in every instrument - every instrument's microphone will pick up a bit of every other instrument. Your band has to be very well rehearsed to do this!

The second method of recording is individual tracking. This is where every part is recorded one at a time and layered on top of each other. The benefits of recording this way are that you can get a pure signal for each instrument, and there won't be any problems with bleed.

You can also easily add recordings from other studios if the musicians you are using are spread out across the world.

Control Room and Live Room

Studios are usually split into two rooms, the control room and the live room. The Control Room is where you and the engineer spend most of your time, it has the mixing desk, monitors, computer etc. The Live Room is where the noise is made - this is where your amplifiers will be, the drummer, the singer etc.

When it comes to recording guitars, if you are recording individually, you'll want the guitar head and effects in the control room, and the speaker cabinet in the live room. Studios will have cables going through the wall that you can use to send the signal from your head to the cab.

This will allow you to twiddle the amplifier settings and effects and perform, without destroying your ears from your amplifier going full whack. This also allows you to push a valve amplifier - valves tend to sound best when they are turned up loud.

The Recording Process

There are a few steps to the recording process, so let's cover them one at a time:

Composition

This is when you are composing your music. You are figuring out what notes to use, the structure for the song, what the lyrics will be if you are going to have lyrics, the instrumentation, etc.

Once you have your notes on a page (or computer file), you are ready for the next step.

Demos

This is creating a rough recording of your song, using whatever you have available at home. This is sometimes done in tandem with the composition stage - if you are writing riffs etc using your guitar, you will probably be recording them as you go.

Things don't need to be perfect at this stage, you are just getting everything recorded so you can get a rough idea of what your song will sound like.

Tracking

This is when you start working on the final recording. You go through each instrument one at a time and take care to get a great recording for each part.

One effective method is to record in sections - record the rhythm guitar for the verse, then the chorus, etc. If you can record the song in one go, do that! You can record each section 2-3 times, then use the comping tool to select the best bits from each take.

Your engineer may do some editing at this level, as you go.

Mixing

Once everything has been recorded, it is time for mixing. Mixing is the art of making the music that you have recorded "fit" together. This involves things like:

- Adding effects
- EQing instruments
- Setting the stereo balance
- Setting levels
- Adding any volume automation and fades

This stage can take several days and cost as much as the recording. A single song can take a few hours to a day or two to mix, an album can take a week or two to mix.

Mastering

This is the final stage in the audio creation of your music and involves fine-tuning the EQ and effects at a song level. The mastering engineer will take a stereo mix of your song (so they will have two channels, left and right) and create fine adjustments with EQ, compression and other effects.

Mastering requirements will vary depending on the medium in which the song will be consumed, for example, vinyl, radio and MP3 all have slightly different mastering requirements.

Marketing

How are you going to promote the song once it is done? Are you going to promote it at all? This can be anything from making a video of you playing the song at home and putting it on youtube, to concerts or paid ads online.

Whatever your project, I would recommend at least making a play-along video at home.

If you went to a studio, you can make a play-along video in the studio, or take a few cameras and make a studio music video. This is something I didn't do when recording Impetuous Desire, which was a huge mistake.

Release

Everything is finally finished and it's time to release your song - congratulations, this is a huge achievement. I guess it's time to get started on the next one…

Preparing for a Studio Session

When preparing for a studio recording session, you want to "plan out" the song for the engineer. The engineer will want to set up the project on their DAW - this means entering the time signature, and time signature changes. They may want to add project markers to show the song sections (remember, this person won't know your songs as you do).

You can prepare all of this information beforehand to make their job as easy as possible - remember, the easier the engineer's job is, the more brain power they can put into helping you record as well as possible, rather than putting their brain power into getting lost between verses and choruses.

You will want to make a list of:

- Song name
- Tempo
- Time signature
- Sections and lengths in bars
- Any changes in time signature or tempo and the bar at which that happens

As an example, here is a song sheet I created for recording Impetuous Desire (I made one of these for every song):

Song: The Path
Tempo: 140bpm
Time Signature 4/4

Structure:
Intro: 8 bars
Verse 1: 16 bars
Chorus: 8 bars
Re-intro: 8 bars
Verse 2: 16 bars
Chorus: 8 bars
Re-intro: 8 bars
Break: 1 bar
Bridge 1: 24 bars
Bridge 2: 8 bars
Re-intro / solo 1: 8 bars
Outro / solo 2: 12 bars

We spent a few minutes at the start of the session putting this info into Cubase and then got busy recording. You may not need all of this information, but it's always better to have this information to hand and not need it than need it and not have it.

You will also want to make sure that your equipment is ready. At the least, this means getting new strings on your guitar, and getting it set up would be better. Get new batteries for your pedals and if your amp has any problems get that seen to before you go to the studio.

Take spares of everything, you don't want to be halfway through a recording session and have a string break, meaning you have to stop to go buy a new string.

You'll also want new picks - new picks will have a slightly sharper edge than a used pick, giving you better contact with the string.

In addition to preparing the song sheets, you'll want to practice recording yourself at home. Before you go to a recording studio, simulate the experience at home and practice recording your songs.

Record your album, then delete it (or copy and paste the DAW session) and do it again.

This way when you get to the recording studio, you'll be confident in your ability to perform.

Another trick you may find useful is to practice the songs you are going to play 5%-10% faster than you want to record them. Your ability on any given day fluctuates, so being able to play the songs faster than you need to gives you some leeway with your ability.

Section 8: Techniques for Being More Creative with Specific Musical Ideas

We have covered a lot of ground on practice, study and general approaches to improving your playing; let's look at some specific techniques you can use to be more creative.

One of the biggest roadblocks to creativity that people face is "the blank page", staring at a blank piece of paper and thinking "well what do I do now?".

The first thing to do in this situation is to give yourself a set of limitations. Decide on the:

- Form.
- Key.
- Harmony and harmonic progressions.
- Type of melody (fast, lyrical, ornamented etc).

Once you have those constraints, the music usually writes itself, all you have to do is take the theory you have learned from studying and apply it to solving the problem that you have outlined for yourself.

Also, you don't have to stick to these constraints. If you use these constraints to get started, but find the music going somewhere different, go with it and see where the music takes you.

A good way to unlock a new source of creativity is to take a different approach to the order in which you compose parts for instruments. For example, guitar players tend to compose the guitar part first, and everything else in the song is structured around the guitar part.

What if you tried writing a bass riff first? Or lyrics? Or a vocal melody? Or a drum pattern?

You will find that by composing for different instruments, your mind will be forced to work a bit differently from usual, and as a result, you will come up with new and interesting ideas.

Here are a few ideas on specific areas of composition that you can use to help you write more ideas. Hopefully, these also show why knowing a little theory can be a powerful thing:

Melody

When it comes to writing melodies, there are a few approaches that we can take. Before deciding on an approach, it's worth thinking about the type of melody that you want to compose, do you want to compose a:

- song melody
- motivic melody
- chant melody
- virtuosic melody

Arpeggiating a Chord Progression

One approach to composing music is to start with a theoretical model, which gets expanded upon before "realising" the music.

Let's say that we had constructed the following model:

And we wanted some ideas on how to arpeggiate it. Sometimes a student will get stuck at this stage - what note in the melody do I start with? Where do I go from there? The terror of the blank page has struck again!

However, if we create a graphical representation of what we are dealing with, we can quickly, in seconds, create dozens of variations.

Each chord in the above model has a top note, middle note and bass note. We could represent this on the following diagram (I call this diagram an arpeggiation map):

We can then simply draw a line to represent how we want to move between the bass, middle and top notes:

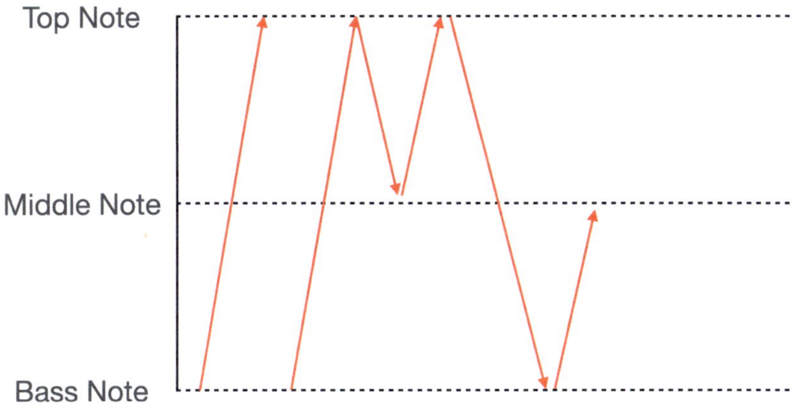

Which would give us the following melody:

If you are unsure how we went from the diagram to the notated arpeggiation, match up the notes in the chord (top stave) with the red lines in the arpeggiation map.

Drawing lines on an arpeggiation map is pretty easy. You could probably make a dozen or so of those in under 2 minutes. You can then translate those into all sorts of arpeggiations of your model. You can then add non-harmonic tones or edit the rhythm as you see fit.

Non-harmonic Tone and Rhythm First Approach to Melody

An alternative approach to composing melodic ideas is to focus instead on the rhythm and type of non-harmonic tones that you want to use in the melody.

Let's assume that we want to write a melody that is one bar long. Choose a time signature, then write out rhythms that fill up a bar. Let's use 4/4. Here is an example of four rhythms we could use:

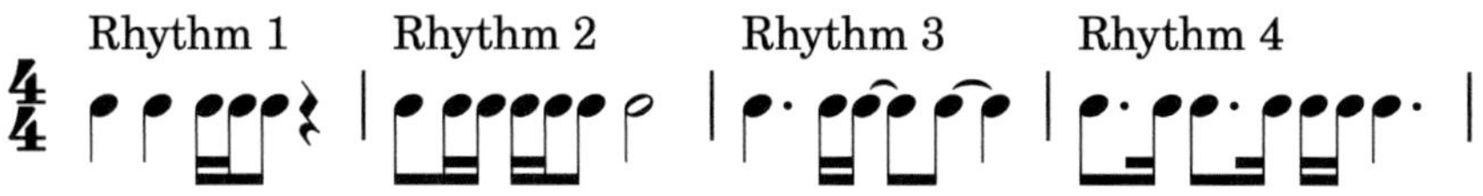

Let's then choose four different ways we can combine pairs of non-harmonic tones:

- Passing tones and neighbour tones
- Reaching tones and neighbour tones
- Reaching tones and escape tones
- Passing tones and reaching tones

Let's assume that we are playing over an Am harmony, and then we can then match up the pairs of non-harmonic tones with different rhythms as follows:

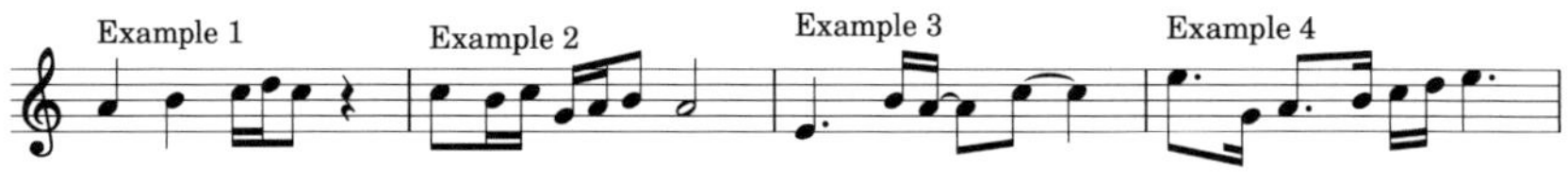

There are a couple of things to note here:

1. These examples are just one possible example. We could have found dozens of ways to combine these rhythms and non-harmonic tones.
2. Example 3 only contains a reaching tone - there were not enough notes to add an escape tone. If things don't work out exactly, that's ok.

Earlier in the book we talked about two ideas:

1. The importance of studying theory.
2. How creativity can be seen as a way of combining theoretical ideas.

Hopefully, these examples are starting to illustrate how easy it can be to be creative when you have studied the theory in depth, and when then start creating scenarios in which to apply it.

Vocal Approach to Melody Writing

A great way to approach melody writing, especially for instrumental music, is to use your voice to compose the melody. It's easy to get very self-conscious when using your voice, so try and find somewhere where you are by yourself to try this out, or hum (it's easier to hum a pitch correctly than it is to sing it).

Take a simple chord progression, loop it, and then use your voice to improvise a melody over the chords.

I approached the song "Longing" on Impetuous Desire this way. I wrote a simple chord progression on guitar, I think it was just two chords. Then looped them, and hummed random notes until I found the note I wanted. That was the first note on the cello. I then restarted the loop, hummed the first note and then hummed to other notes until I found the next note that fitted. I now had two notes.

And so on and so on, until I had the entire melody.

You can apply this to guitar melodies, using this method to compose the fundamental notes of the melody. You can then, if you want, make the melody more complex by changing how those notes are ornamented, adding arpeggios and scale ideas around those fundamental pitches.

This is a great way to get a highly melodic melody.

Warning on Melody Writing

This first time guitar players approach writing melodies, they, more often than not, add too many notes. They end up with ideas that are musical diarrhoea, with straight 16th notes everywhere.

This often comes from insecurity around the perceived complexity of the idea. Remember, melodies do not need to be complex to be enjoyable. Sure, write a complex melody, IF it serves the music. But don't add notes for the sake of it.

If you find you always write melodies in straight 16ths (or something similar), try challenging yourself by restricting yourself to different types of rhythms. The "non-harmonic tone and rhythm first approach" that is outlined above would be a great exercise for you.

Using your voice to improvise a melody would also be a great exercise, as the voice cannot sing as fast as we can play on guitar.

Writing Chord Progressions and Strumming Patterns

Free Writing Chord Progressions for a Song

We're writing a song, and songs have a structure. So to get started, let's make up a simple structure:

Verse

Chorus

Verse

Chorus

Bridge

Chorus

Let's start by restricting ourselves to a particular key, say, E minor. Let's first look at the chords in E minor:

Em F#dim G Am Bm C D

We'll ignore possible chromatic chords, modal mixture and other minor chords, restricting ourselves to the natural minor scale outlined above.

To make things easier for ourselves, let's also ignore the F#dim chord, which is a bit harder to use.

Ignoring the F#dim leaves us with six chords:

Em G Am Bm C D

Now, let's take four of these chords at random (pick four different chords to what I choose so that you can see this method works for yourself):

Chord Progression 1: Em - C - G - Am

Let's repeat that process to write a second chord progression:

Chord Progression 2: C - Bm - Em - C

Finally, let's write a third chord progression that is only two chords long, but we'll have each chord last two bars:

Chord Progression 3: Am - Am - D - D

Next, we need some rhythms that we can use with these chord progressions. Let's use a mixture of eighth notes and quarter notes:

Rhythm 1

Rhythm 2

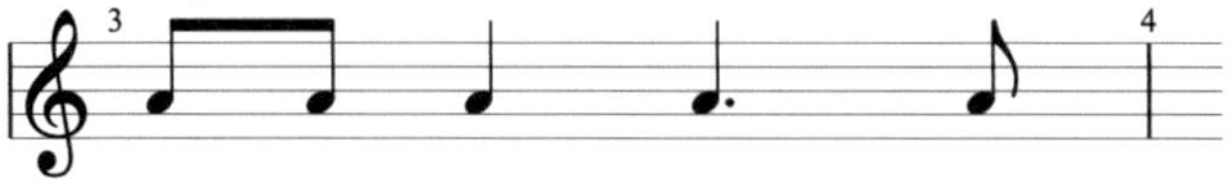

Rhythm 3

Ignore the pitches, here we are solely concerned with the rhythm

We'll use Chord Progression 1 and Rhythm 1 as a Verse, Chord Progression 2 and Rhythm 2 as a Chorus, and Chord Progression 3 and Rhythm 3 as a Bridge, and hey presto, we now have a song:

Song

Music by Sam Russell

Sure, it might not be the greatest song in the world… but it's a start. And it wasn't exactly difficult to write. And most importantly… it sounds like a song!

Once you have a basic outline as we have above, you can then start picking at it, deciding what you like, what you don't like, and editing it into a song that you do like.

Using Functional Harmony to Write Chord Progressions

The Common Practice Period (CPP) is an era of music that most people know as Classical Music. It was when great composers, such as Mozart and Beethoven were alive.

One of the conventions that was followed for writing harmonic progressions (what guitar players often understand as chord progressions) is called "Functional Harmony". This is a method for deciding "what chord comes next".

To give a very brief overview (there is a lot, lot more to functional harmony which warrants an entire course), we use numerals to "label" the chords from the major scale:

C major:	C	Dm	Em	F	G	Am	B°
Numeral:	I	ii	iii	IV	V	vi	vii°

Note: Numerals give us a way to analyse chord progressions by looking at the relationship of a chord to its scale, rather than the chord by itself. For example, using numerals, we can think of Dm as being the second chord in a C major scale, rather than thinking of it as the pitches D, F and A.

The chord numerals are then organised into Tonic, Sub-dominant and Dominant:

Tonic (T)		**Sub-Dominant (S)**		**Dominant (D)**	
I	vi	IV	ii	vii°	V

Generally speaking, we move from left to right through the table. We can skip chords when moving right. We can only move left when moving from D to T. For example:

Chord Progression 1: I - vi - IV - ii - vii° - V - I

Chord Progression 2: I - ii - V - I

Chord Progression 3: I - vi - IV - V

If you take your guitar and try playing these progressions, you should find that have quite a structured/logical/classical sound to them, especially if you pay attention to the voice leading.

Are you starting to see the benefits of in-depth study now? When you understand functional harmony, voice leading and form; composing can almost be boiled down to following some rules, creating some progressions and then filling in the gaps with some notes.

Now, there is a lot, lot more to functional harmony than this, but as I mentioned before, that would be an entire course and outside the scope of this book.

We could use functional harmony combined with the rhythm and structure ideas from the previous example to write a song:

Chord Progression 1: I - vi - IV - ii - vii° - V - I

C major: C - Am - F - Dm - B° - G - C

Chord Progression 2: I - ii - V - I

C major: C - Dm - G - C

Chord Progression 3: I - vi - IV - V

C major: C - Am - F - G

Which would give us the following song:

Song Using Functional Harmony

Music by Sam Russell

Again, from here we can start editing to get it more the way we want it, or adding to the structure, other instruments, etc.

Improvised Ideas When Writing

Usually, most guitarists approach songwriting by improvising ideas on their guitar. Why not put your improvisational skills to use in a different medium?

You could try starting with a bass guitar and improvising a bass idea, then arrange the guitar and drums around your bass idea.

You could try starting by writing a cool drum pattern that you then write guitar and bass over.

Maybe you start with a vocal melody (or work with a singer) and then compose around the vocals?

Putting your improvisation skills to work with different instruments (even if you aren't very good at them) will quickly give you new ideas that you work with for your songwriting.

I would strongly recommend buying a bass guitar, even if it's a cheap one (mine was £100), they are great for coming up with ideas and also for making demos of your musical ideas.

Principles Behind the Above Creativity Ideas

The above ideas are great, but what is important is that you understand the principle behind the ideas, so that you can not only use these creativity tools effectively, but create your own.

We are taking a specific element of music, whether it's chord tone melodies, chord progressions, rhythm in melody, etc; thinking of several variations of that aspect of music, then taking those variations and "fleshing them out" into complete ideas.

You can also see how important it is to have a good grasp of music theory, and how understanding music theory can immensely aid creativity.

Section 9: Final Thoughts on Creativity

Can Anyone Learn Anything?

We've spent an entire book discussing how you can become more creative. But are there any limits on the levels you can reach, or on the levels of creative achievement that people can reach in general?

The answer is: Sort of.

This has a bit to do with IQ. One thing that IQ affects is the speed at which someone can learn and understand complex information. To put it another way, someone with a high IQ can learn complex things quickly. Someone with a low IQ will take a long time to learn complex things.

I believe anyone with an average or even below-average IQ can become an expert at something over the course of their life.

Only people with high IQs will be able to become experts in multiple fields over the course of their life. This is due to the practical limit of how long we live. The rate at which we learn, the time we spend learning and the length of our lives determine the number of fields in which we can become an expert. And we only have so much time.

It's also worth noting that IQ can be increased - learning is simply recognising how concepts fit together. If you can train your mind to think more conceptually, you can increase your IQ.

If you've managed to read this far in the book, you have enough intelligence to become an expert-level guitarist/composer.

When considering this, it is also important to factor in time. If you do take a long time to learn something, but you increase the time you spend each day on it, then you will learn as fast, or even faster, than someone who is theoretically more intelligent.

The old idiom of "Hard work beats talent when talent doesn't work hard" has some truth to it!

The First Four Hours of Your Day Define Your Life

I have a pet theory I've been considering over the last couple of years: The first four hours of your day define your life. The first four hours of your day are your best time of day, your brain is alert and you can focus for extended periods.

The most effective way to get better at guitar and writing music is to wake up and spend your morning working on it. Now, doing 4 hours might be difficult if you have a job. But if you can, go to bed earlier and wake up earlier, so you can put an hour or two into music.

You will see that you improve quickly.

I wanted to write this book, so the first 1-2 hours of my day for the last few months have been put into writing this book, followed by a couple of hours of guitar practice.

If the guitar and music are something you want to work on full-time, you will have to figure out a way to either make more money with less time or make money from playing the guitar.

Progress is Not Accidental

Hopefully, now you are starting to see that:

1) Progress is not accidental

2) Great guitarists are not born, they are made

Every great guitarist has a story about the hours and hours of practice time they put into their instrument. If you replicate that, you will replicate the results.

Practice doesn't magically happen, it has to be planned, scheduled and prioritised in your life.

Creativity as a Path to Happiness

Is it possible to be too happy? What do we mean when we talk about happiness? We're not talking about some drug-like state of deliriousness, but more a state of satisfaction or contentedness that runs through our lives, like a backing track.

Human beings survive via production - this is an unavoidable fact of life. When you can spend your productive time, or at least some of it, creating something you love, you will gain a piece of happiness.

A fundamental part of being human is problem-solving. Some writers have described man as a teleological being - this means "goal orientated". Setting yourself a challenge and then overcoming it is a fundamental part of being human, and when we act in accordance with our nature we tend to feel good.

Composing, recording and releasing a piece of music takes a lot of work. Composing a piece of music is an incredible feat of problem-solving. It involves pushing your mind to see what it's capable of, and then concretising a range of concepts so you can create a physical representation of what your mind can do (by physical we mean existing in a format that others can perceive).

As such, I believe that taking guitar seriously and creating music can be a great way to be happier. I certainly find that I'm at my happiest when creating and recording music.

Conclusion

That's about everything I have to say about practising the guitar more effectively, learning effectively and becoming a more creative guitarist.

Thank you for reading, and I hope you got some useful ideas out of this book that will help you improve your life.

If you want more information, resources and courses, then check out www.study-guitar.com for the latest updates.

Appendix

Here are a few guides and lists of useful things. Some of these are things I have personally used, and some are things I have not used but that you may find useful.

Appendix 1: Sample Libraries / Sound Libraries

These are a great way to get more realism in your demos and can also be used in final releases. Some people like to compose directly with sound libraries.

Sound libraries are pre-recorded instruments. For example, someone will record all the notes that a violin can play, then you program your DAW, via MIDI, and it plays back the notes you programmed using the pre-recorded violin.

Libraries can take up huge amounts of space, not only for storage but in your RAM. You will probably need an external hard drive to store the libraries you use and you may need to upgrade your RAM.

Some libraries include a "player". This is the software that stitches together sound samples based on the parts you have written. Some libraries do not include the player and are just samples. These libraries require a third-party player to work. The most common third-party player is Kontakt:

https://www.native-instruments.com/en/products/komplete/samplers/kontakt-6/

Orchestral Sample Libraries

Orchestral libraries require some knowledge of MIDI programming to get the most out of them. You will have to learn how to program velocity and a couple of MIDI CC channels to get them working as well as possible. I would advise watching reviews of libraries on YouTube, reading the manual for libraries you get and you may even consider finding someone to give a few lessons on how to program effectively.

Bigcat

If you want a free library, there is a guy called "bigcat" who has done a vocal library here: https://plugins4free.com/plugin/2888/
There is also an orchestral library here: https://plugins4free.com/dev/514/, both of which can be downloaded for free.

EastWest Composer Cloud

This is a $20/mo subscription that gives you access to nearly the entire EW library. This is what I use. https://www.soundsonline.com/composercloud. It is one of the best libraries available.

EW Symphonic Orchestra

EW Symphonic Orchestra is $400, and while that is a big chunk of change, it's at the lower end of the price spectrum for tools like this. From a "Dollars for sound quality" perspective it's probably the best-priced option. This library is included in EW Composer Cloud.

Spitfire BBC Orchestra

Spitfire offers a limited version of one of their libraries for £49:
https://www.spitfireaudio.com/bbcso/
I have mixed feelings about this, great price point, and a limited choice of articulations. But if all you want is some nice sustained strings and a few horns here and there, it could work for you. You can also apply to them to get it for free (I think one of my students did this).

Other Libraries

The other big libraries are Vienna Symphonic Library (https://www.vsl.co.at/en), Orchestral Tools (https://www.orchestraltools.com/store/home) and CineSamples (https://

cinesamples.com) all of which are quite pricey, but these are things composers use in movies and TV shows. These are top-level pro libraries.

StaffPad Libraries

If you are going to use StaffPad for composing, it has libraries broken into orchestral sections (strings, woodwinds, brass, percussion) and priced at $80 each (roughly). They also have pianos, harps, harpsichords, church organs and a few other instruments (including guitar).

Other things...

Some libraries require the Kontakt player from Native instruments:
https://www.native-instruments.com/en/products/komplete/samplers/kontakt-6/library/
The player comes with (I think!) some orchestral samples, but I don't know how they stand up against the other big names. One of the nice things about EastWest libraries is that they have their own player.

Rock / Drum Sample Libraries

Rock and drum sample libraries tend to be a bit more "out of the box" than orchestral tools, as the dynamics involves are not as complex, but most will still benefit from some programming.

When it comes to rock, pop and metal, a company called Toontrack is dominating company the industry: https://www.toontrack.com

Logic Pro Drummer

It's worth noting that Logic Pro comes with a pretty good built-in drum sample library. Their drummer tool can automatically create drum beats for you. You can drag the drummer file to a different

MIDI track and have a different library playback the drums part Logic created.

Most DAWs come with semi-decent built-in drum samples.

East West Ministry of Rock

This has a collection of drums, bass guitars and guitars. This is a nice all-rounder to give your demos some more realism. It's included in EW Composer Cloud.

https://www.soundsonline.com/guitars-and-bass/ministry-of-rock-1

I've used the bass guitars a lot when creating demos and backing tracks for myself.

Toontrack EZ Drummer

This is a great "goto" drum library. It's hard to go wrong with this.

https://www.toontrack.com/product/ezdrummer-3/

Toontrack Superior Drummer

This is the big brother to EZ Drummer, giving incredible sound control and programming options.

https://www.toontrack.com/product/superior-drummer-3/

Superior Drummer is more than a sample library, it is a full drum production DAW in a plugin (that can also be run independently to your DAW).

GetGoodDrums

This is the brainchild of Nolly and Matt from the band Periphery. Their libraries are quite cheap as they use Kontakt player. They also offer some presets for a Kemper.

https://www.getgooddrums.com

Appendix 2: Books Worth Studying

Writing Better Lyrics - Pat Pattison

This is a great introduction to lyric writing, going in-depth into several techniques and approaches, with exercises to get your lyric writing skills up to scratch.

Orchestration - Walter Piston

This book is a classic, giving a comprehensive overview of the instruments in an orchestra and also different musical textures that can be created with those instruments.

Harmony - Walter Piston

A good, although sometimes complex, overview of common practice period harmony and how it works. A great introduction to composing more in-depth with the CPP approach.

Guitar Secrets - Joe Satriani

This is a collection of articles that Joe Satriani wrote for a guitar magazine way back. It's a great insight into his mind with good exercises to work on.

Rock Discipline - John Petrucci

This is a legendary book with exercises to work on developing your rock guitar technique.

Counterpoint - Alfred Mann / J Fux

This book is a foundation of western music theory practice and was studied by Beethoven and Mozart. The book has a unique approach, written in the style of a lecture from a master to a student. Written by J Fux and translated by Alfred Mann. Some things are poorly explained (or not explained at all), but it is a good starting point for anyone with a serious interest in music theory.

AB Guide to Music Theory, vol 1 - Eric Taylor

This book is a fantastic introduction to music theory and I would strongly recommend it to everyone getting started with music theory. It is probably the best introduction to music theory I've seen.

Introduction to Tonal Theory - Peter Westergaard

This is probably the densest and most in-depth book on the technical aspects of composition I have ever read. I am still only 25% through the book. It's out of print and quite expensive to find a copy. If you want a serious deep dive into tonal music, this is one of the greatest books on the subject.

Appendix 3: Pick and String Recommendations

My personal favourites are Ernie Ball Super Slinky Cobalt 9 gauge strings. The picks I like best are Dunlop Flow 1.5mm max grip - these are just right for rock and metal playing.

Appendix 4: Setting Up Metronomes to Practice

I've chosen three different exercises that look at three different areas of guitar playing, to try and provide enough musical situations so that you can make good decisions when programming your metronome.

Chord Playing Exercises

Let's say we are working on the following chord exercise:

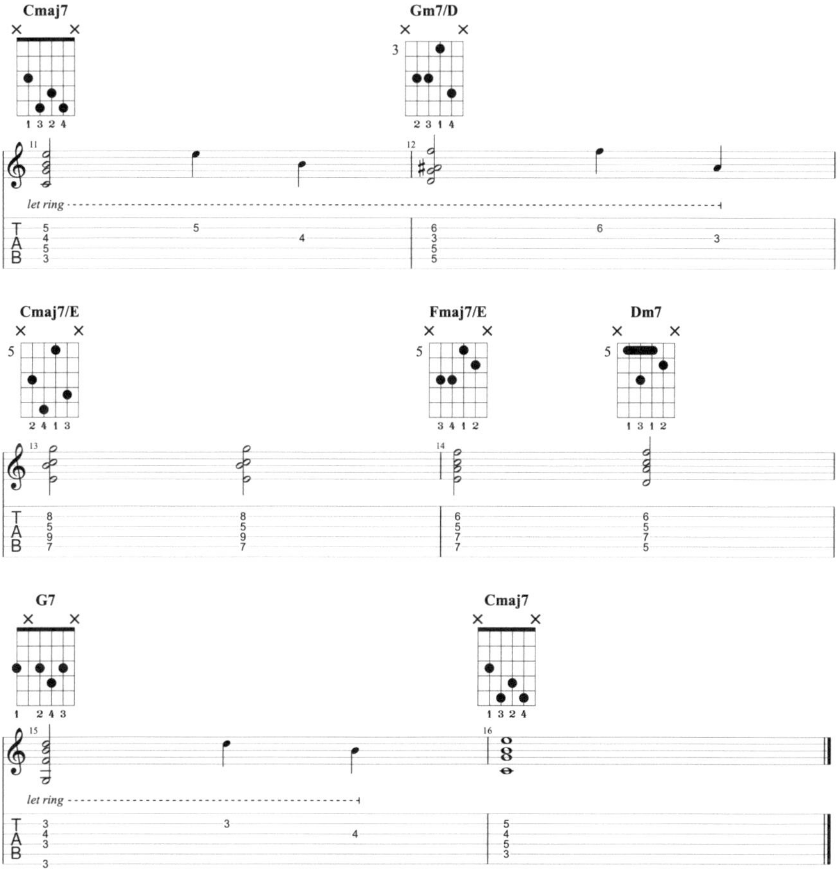

What are some important features of this exercise that we need to think about when programming our metronome?

1. Subdivisions. The smallest subdivision that is being used is a quarter note, so we need to ensure the metronome is counting the quarter note.
2. Chord changes every bar. We will want to make sure the metronome is counting the start of every bar.

Programming Soundbrenner for Practising Chords

When practising this exercise, I would set up Soundbrenner as follows:

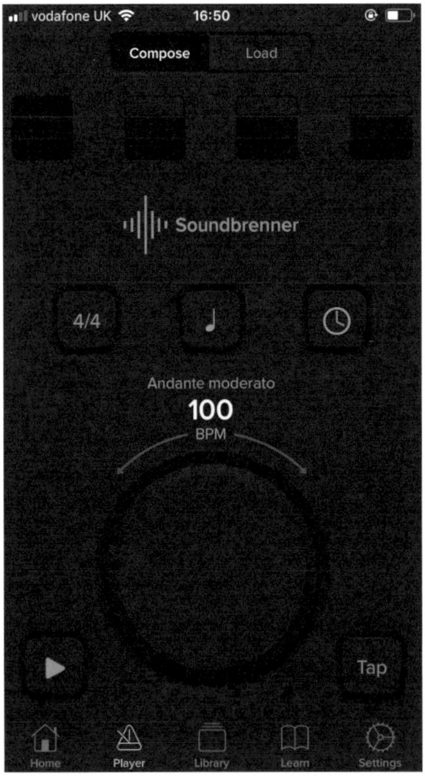

You can see that the middle button is set to count quarter notes and that the first beat (the beats are counted by the squares at the top) is set differently to the following three beats.

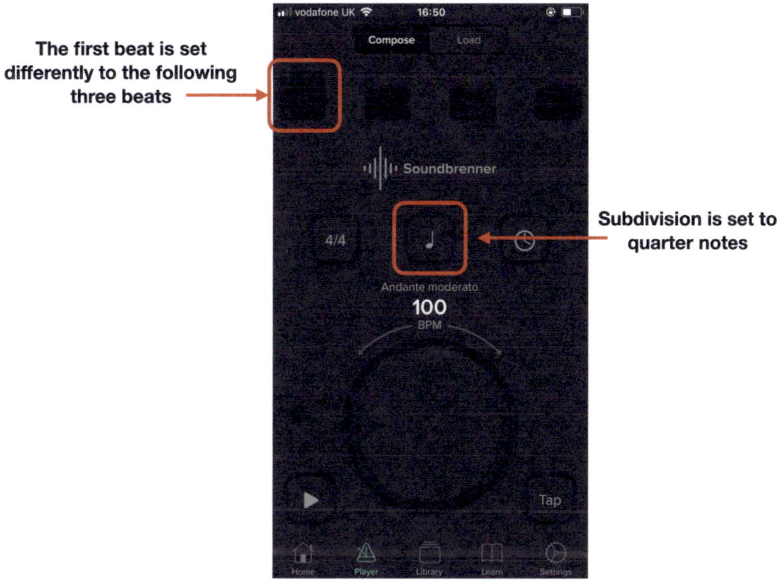

Programming a Guitar Pro Drum Track for Practising Chord Changes

In the following examples, we'll use Guitar Pro to create a custom drum metronome for this exercise.

We have the same requirements that we looked at for soundbrenner: we want to count the quarter note subdivision and count the start of the bar.
Additionally, we will write the count on the metronome track, so we can count out loud while practising.

Add a drum track and set the score to "multi-track view". Then program the drums with something simple to count the beats and the start of the bar like this:

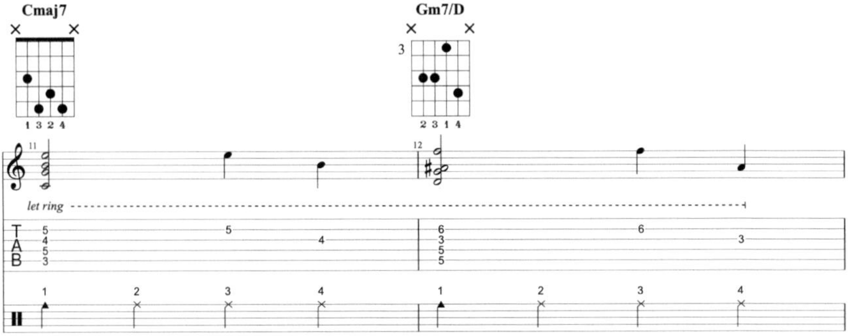

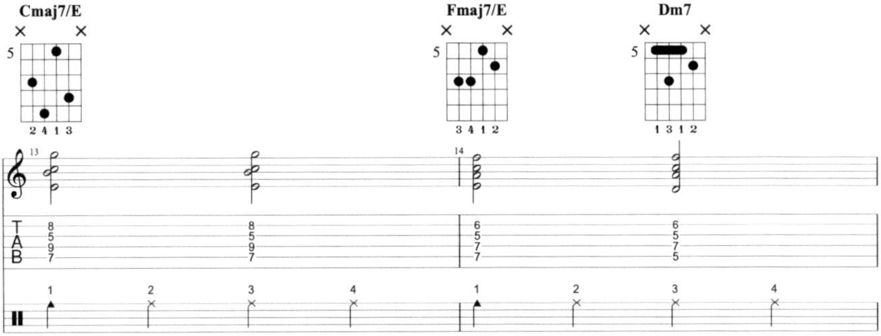

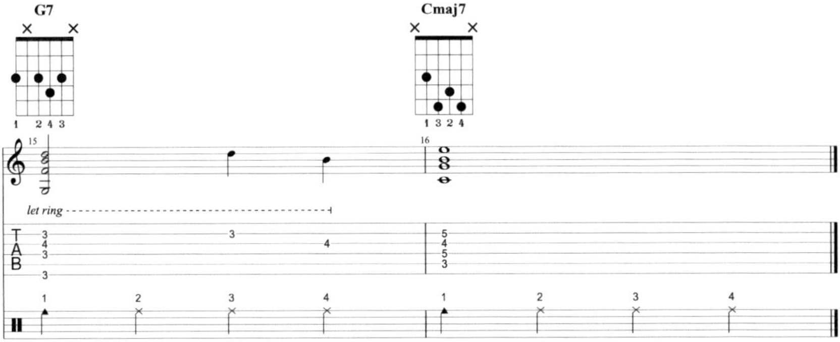

If you put the cursor on each drum note and press “T”, you can enter the count for that particular beat.

As you can see from the above tab, you now know exactly which beat every note in the exercise is on, which makes practising much easier!

Writing the beat on top of the drum part is especially useful if you are new to reading rhythm notation.

Programming a Metronome for an Arpeggio-Based Exercise

The next exercise we'll look at is arpeggio-based:

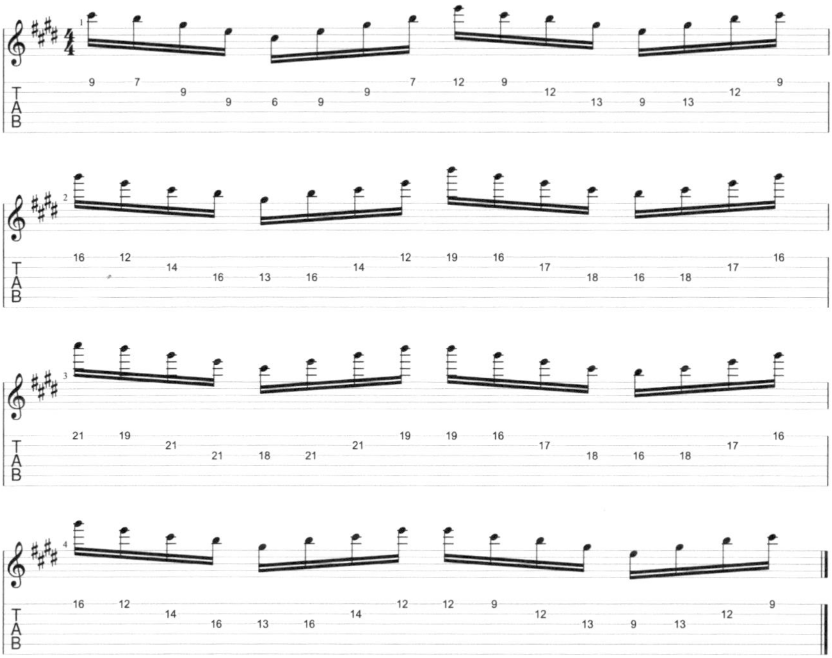

In this exercise, we're playing a C#m7 through all its inversions, ascending the neck and back down again. (You can extend the exercise further down the neck, but for brevity, I've left it as is).

Programming Guitar Pro Drums as a Metronome on Arpeggio-Based Exercises

When I first started working on this, I had the metronome playing a metronome beat as follows:

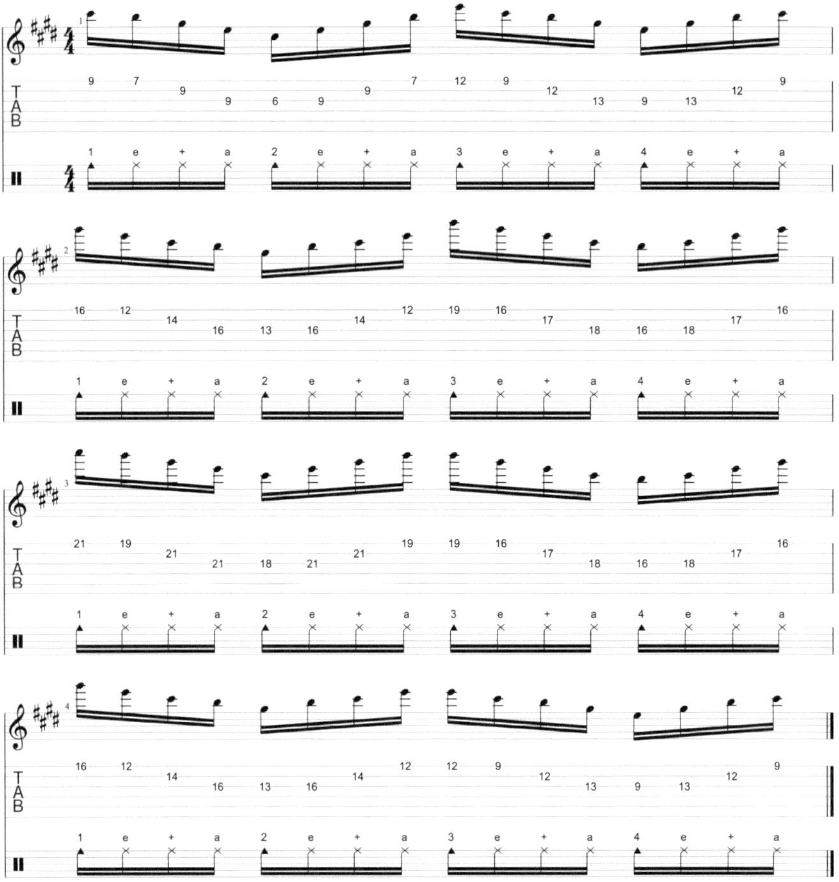

However, I found this slightly problematic. I found myself slipping out of time at higher tempos, especially around the third string. For some reason, I was keeping time nicely when changing positions along the 1st string, with the position changes seeming to act as my timing "anchor".

But that's not good enough, I wanted the entire piece in time, so I changed the metronome slightly, using a different sound for the start of beats 2 and 4:

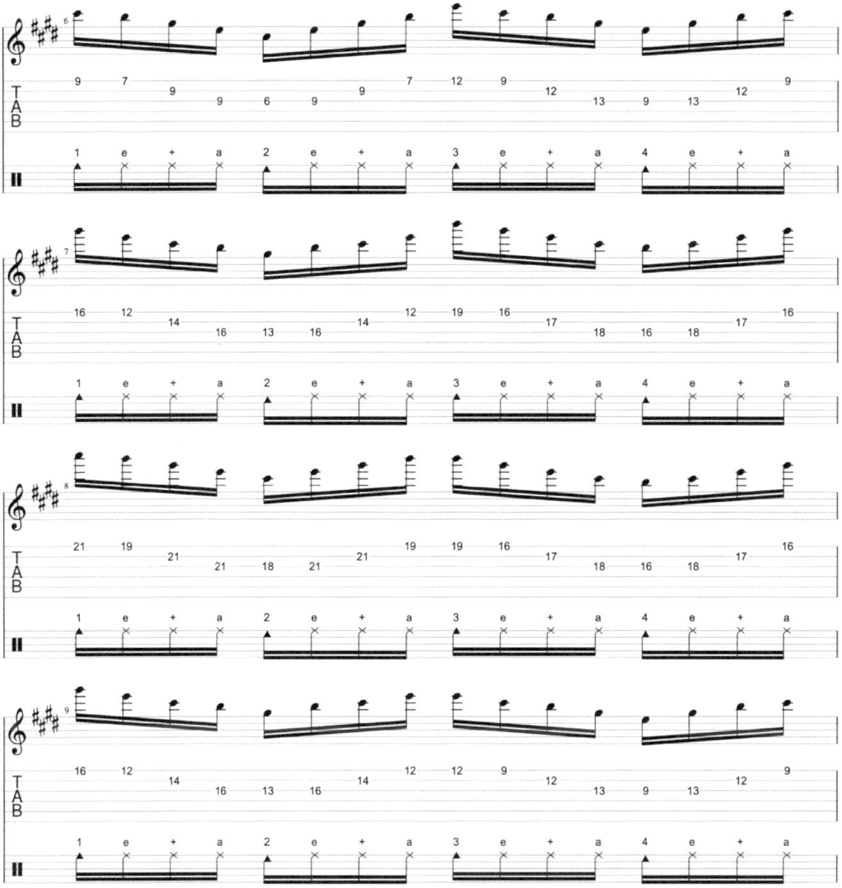

If you look at beats 2 and 4, you can see that the metronome is playing something slightly different.

I found this made it much, much easier to stay in time.
If you find yourself struggling with an arpeggio-based exercise, try setting up your metronome to play different sounds on the inflexion points (where the arpeggio changes direction).

When practising in general, if you find a particular section of an exercise difficult, you can try changing the metronome at that point to help you maintain focus.

Setting Up Soundbrenner for Electric Guitar Arpeggio Exercises

It is quite easy to set up Soundbrenner to do the above exercise. Here is Soundrenner setup for playing straight 16ths, counting the start of each beat and counting the start of the bar (like my drum metronome was originally setup):

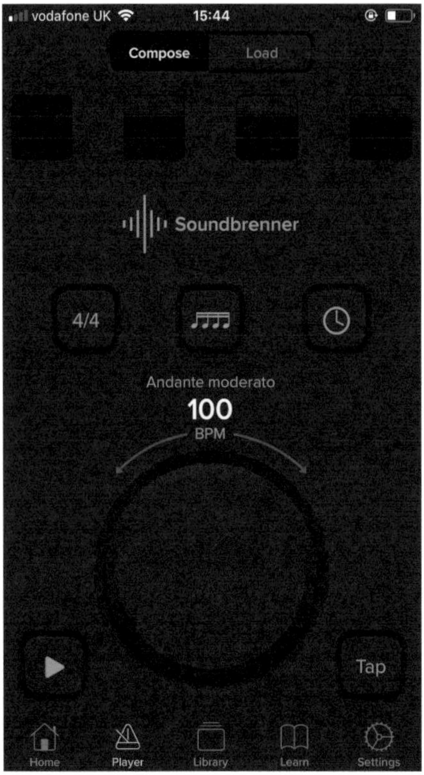

and here we've modified the way Soundbrenner is counting the beat so that we hear beats 1 and 3 differently to 2 and 4:

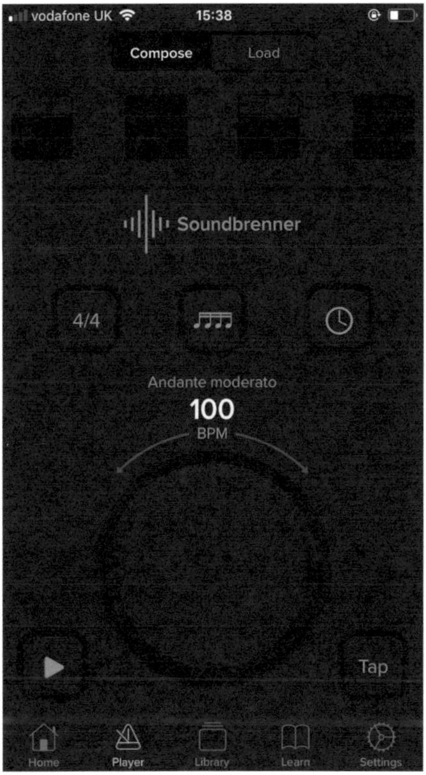

Observe that beats 1 and 3 play a different sound to beats 2 and 4.

This is a small change, but I found it helped. Hopefully, you will also find this beneficial to your practising.

Programming Metronomes for Scale Based Exercises

Here is a pretty standard exercise, working on 3-note per string scales, specifically, the melodic minor scale (which is used a lot in neoclassical guitar playing):

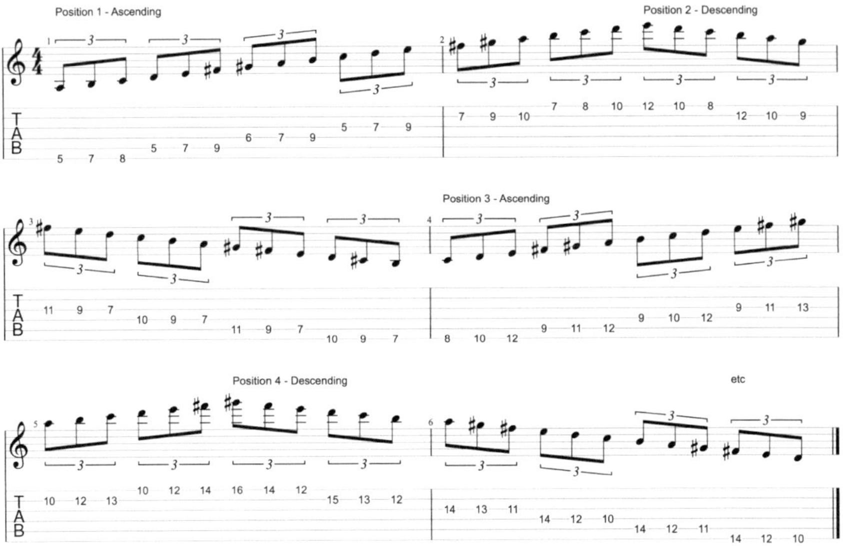

You can see that we are using a 3-note per string melodic minor scale, alternately ascending and descending through scale positions up the neck.

As I previously explained in this article on neoclassical scales for electric guitar, in a classical context the melodic minor scale differs between ascending and descending patterns.

In the above exercise, we are using the scale in a rock context, so the scale is the same ascending and descending.

When practising something like this, the important feature is the start of the beat, which is also the first note on each string.

You can see that the scale pattern lasts 1.5 bars (at least, when in 4/4 it does). We could have written the exercise in 6/4 and were I to revisit this exercise, I would do so.
However, when it comes to setting up the metronome, it does not make a difference if we are in 4/4 or 6/4.

We are not so interested in the start of the bar here, just the start of the beat.

Having said that, if you find that it helps you stay in time better to have the start of each pattern counted on the metronome, you can put the exercise in 6/4 and have the metronome count the start of each bar.

So, to count each beat, here is how I would set up the drums on Guitar Pro and the metronome on Soundbrenner:

Writing a Guitar Pro Drum Metronome for a 3 Note Per String Scale Exercise

We would simply have the drums as follows:

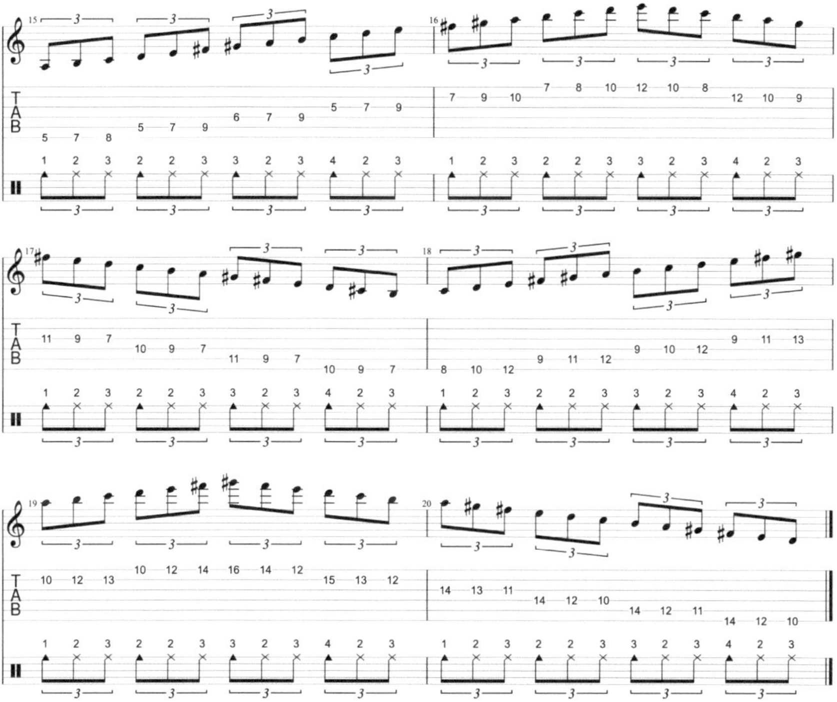

Setting up Sounbrenner for a 3 Note Per String Scale Exercise

You should set up Soundbrenner as follows:

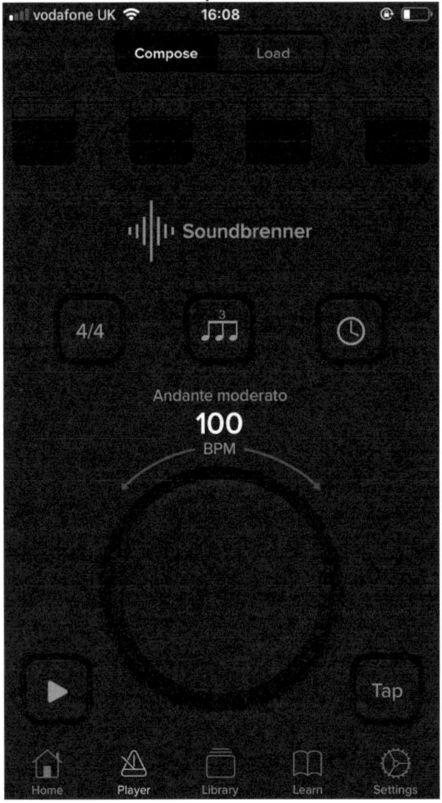

As you can see, the start of each beat is the same, and the subdivision is set to triplet eighth notes.

Appendix 5: How to Hold the Guitar

As a beginner, you want to get started in a seated position with the guitar. Rest your guitar on the same side as your fretting hand. If you are playing the frets with your left hand, you want the guitar on your left leg.

You will find it very useful to have a footstool. This will slightly raise your leg, which holds the guitar very comfortably. You will find that, without a footstool, the guitar slides off your leg, or you have to hold the guitar on the opposite leg, which is more uncomfortable and is also bad for your technique and posture, as it twists your back and torso.

How to sit holding an electric guitar.

When sitting with an electric guitar, keep your back straight while sitting towards the edge of your chair.

With footstools, you don't need something mega expensive, but you also don't want something super cheap. Get a foot stool that is either wooden or metal. If you get a metal one, make sure the rubber mat that holds the foot is riveted on - a glued mat will come off. Also, with metal footstools, get an extra strong one. Cheap footstools can collapse/buckle with a little time.

How to Play Notes on the Guitar

Now we have covered some of the basics of the instrument, let's quickly look at the correct way to hold the strings down and play notes on the guitar:

Keep Your Fingers Arched

Beginner guitarists should ensure their fingers are arched while playing - each joint in the finger should be bent (with exceptions).

Thumb Should be Upright on the Back of the Neck

Your thumb should be straight on the back of the neck. pointing towards the ceiling. The joint in the thumb should not be bent.

The wrist Hangs Underneath the Neck

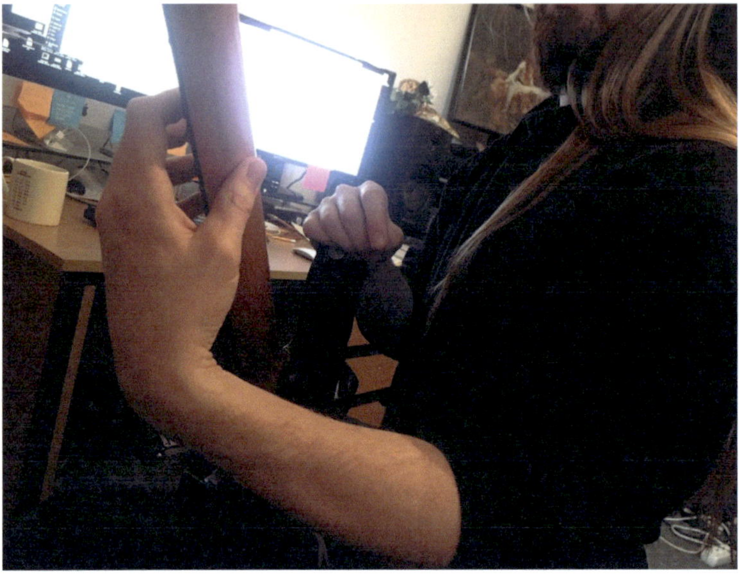

Beginner guitarists need to ensure their wrist hands underneath the guitar neck

Hold the Strings Down With Your Fingertips

Use the tip of your finger, close to the nail. Do not use the pad of your finger to hold down the strings.

Holding down the strings with the pads of your fingers
is a common mistake.

Elbow Stays Close To Your Body

Elbow should hand loose next to the body.

Here the arm is too tense causing the elbow to move away from the body. Do not do this!

How to Hold a Guitar Pick

Here is a simple two-step process on how to hold a guitar pick:

Step 1: Rest the pick on the side of your first finger
Your finger should be parallel to the centre axis of the pick. Leave around 1/3 of the pick sticking out past your first finger:

Step 2: Gently grip the pick with your thumb
Take your thumb, and place the pad of your thumb on top of the grip, roughly perpendicular to your first finger:

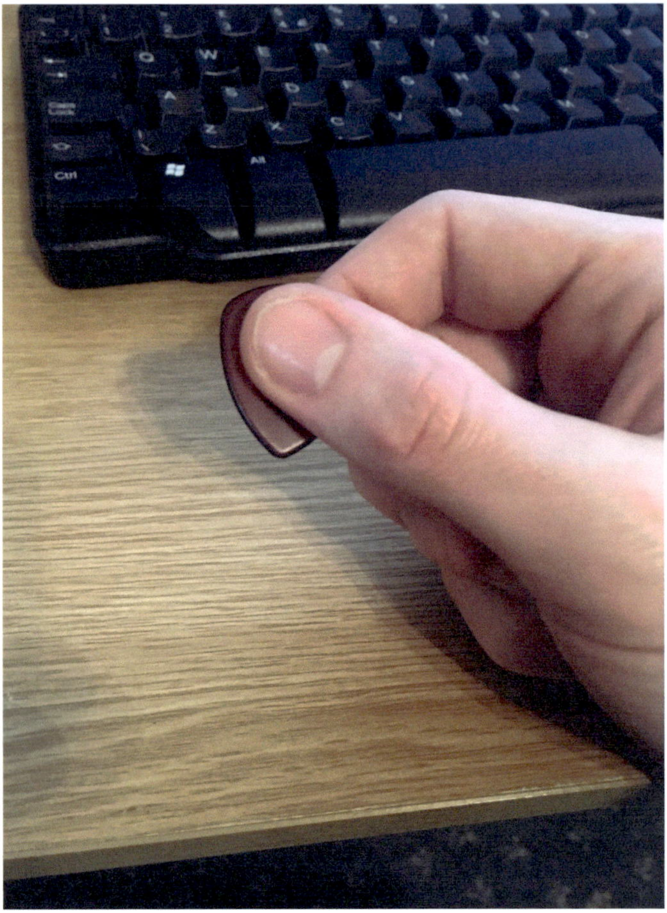

Appendix 6: Useful Software

This is a list of programs that I have found useful over the years.

Guitar Pro

This is the best guitar tablature writing program available. It prioritises tab entry over notation entry but is capable of both. You can create beautiful and clear tabs, and parts for all instruments and play them back.

You can add scale, arpeggio and chord diagrams to your tabs.

Playback sounds aren't great, I usually use the clean sound for all guitar parts because it sounds nicer than the distortion sound. Orchestral instruments can sound pretty bad.

Musescore

This is a free program. Musescore is mainly designed for orchestral instruments but can handle guitar tabs. Working in guitar tab does take some setting up (not much) which is not intuitive, but there are tutorials on how to do this.

Musescore does not have as many tab features as Guitar Pro, but it has enough to make a good tab. It has a nice feature where you can "drag" notes between strings, which makes re-arranging parts for the guitar very fast.

Musescore has good tab entry and great notation entry features. Using Musescore is a bit more complex than Guitar Pro.

Musescore also has a nice feature where you can "break" a score up, inserting text boxes between sections of music. This is great for teachers who want to create worksheets for students.

The default orchestral sounds are much better than Guitar Pro.

Logic Pro X (LPX)

This is a DAW. LPX is great for recording music. You can also create quite nice-looking scores and guitar tabs. LPX allows you to record MIDI and audio. You can edit and perform all sorts of functions on both the audio and MIDI. You can play the MIDI back through sample libraries.

Note entry with LPX is done either with drag and drop (dragging and dropping each note, one by one) which is incredibly tedious, or via keyboard input - either using your keyboard as a pseudo piano keyboard or via an external MIDI keyboard.

An external MIDI keyboard is the fastest way to do note entry.

LPX is a great way to do everything you would want to do with music. I use it to write my tabs, record demos, and then record, mix and master the “real thing”.

StaffPad

When it comes to writing orchestral or classical music, StaffPad is fantastic. It is a musical handwriting recognition app, available on iPad or Microsoft Surface. You draw in the notes and StaffPad recognises them.

When working strictly with notation, I have found StaffPad to be the fastest way to work. It has additional libraries for purchase which are incredibly realistic.

Staffpad can export to audio, MIDI, PDF and other formats. Exporting to MIDI or audio means the files can then be imported into LPX - which is great for recording and tabbing the guitar parts!

StaffPad does not do tabs, it is strictly notation only.

Positive Grid BIAS

This is the best software simulation amplifier I have seen. You can run BIAS as an AU or VST inside your DAW, or run it standalone; allowing you to directly connect your guitar to your computer via your sound interface and record your guitar.

This is great for practising or creating demos of your songs.

There are a few effects you can get. The higher-end package allows you to “model” your amplifier - you set up a microphone with your amplifier and BIAS will find the settings to model your amplifier. I’ve had mixed results trying this, it is nowhere near as good as a Kemper for modelling - and also nowhere near the price!